COUNTDOWN
TO CHAOS

COUNTDOWN TO CHAOS

CHICAGO, AUGUST 1968
TURNING POINT IN AMERICAN POLITICS

by
Jeffrey St. John

Editorial Associate, Kathryn L. Boggs

NASH PUBLISHING CORPORATION
LOS ANGELES, CALIFORNIA
1969

*To Alice Widener and Robert Bleiberg
—who told us long before Chicago,
but we wouldn't listen.*

CONTENTS

PREFACE

This work is not just a report on the violent Convention week of the Democratic Party in August 1968. To take such a narrow context, as so many have, is to miss, as well as misread, the historical importance of that week of revolutionary warfare against the American political system. It is this author's judgment that Chicago in August 1968 represented an important turning point in the recent history of the United States. For the first time since the growth of violence and anarchy in the decade of the 1960s, the very political process of America came under violent attack by a revolutionary minority. (I have provided an in-depth study of this movement in *The Anarchy of Young America,* which has a foreword by John Chamberlain.)

The context this work provides is much wider than, say, the Walker Report, which was a study of the week of violence in Chicago for The National Commission on the Causes and Prevention of Violence. Instead, I date the actual planning for the August 1968 Chicago week of violence back to the summer of 1965. It was then that the National Conference for New Politics (NCNP) was created at the Center for the Study of Democratic Institutions, a private foundation which has been the seedbed for many of the ideas employed by the revolutionary New Left in America. The Center, as it is known, is a tax-exempt radical-leftist political organization that Americans should learn more about.

Among the long-range goals of the Center is the creation of a "new constitution" that will guarantee economic and social rights—in the process, ignoring individual rights and their protection by government as set forth by the Founders and framers of the Constitution in 1789. In many ways, the actions of the members of the NCNP, inside and outside of the Convention, were a step leading toward this long-range goal. The violence and disruption at the Chicago Convention were for the purpose of moving both U.S. political parties farther to the political left—with the ultimate goal of going beyond the policies of Franklin Roosevelt and into a radical—

but not new—economic, social, and political order in America.

Chicago Convention week 1968 was the joining of a historic confrontation between the spirit and philosophy of two revolutions of the last two hundred years: the Revolution of 1776, which for the first time in man's history enunciated the set of principles of individualism, economic free enterprise, and rights; and the revolution of 1933, precipitated by Franklin Roosevelt under the New Deal. More precisely, the New Deal was a counterrevolution that, by advocating collectivism, state economic control, and rule by elite, stands in direct opposition to what the Revolution of 1776 created. The activists inside and outside the Democratic Convention who initiated violence and disruption are seeking to complete the radical goals of the 1933 counterrevolution, and, in the process, they hope to destroy the legacy of liberty, individualism, and economic progress. The response of those under attack in Chicago, namely Mayor Richard Daley, was wholly inadequate to deal with the violent assault on the American political process. Mayor Daley did many things wrong, none of which have been clearly spelled out.

The failure of what is called "the establishment" in Chicago and the leaders of the Democratic Party, in a more compelling sense, was their inability to draw a line between civil disobedience and the deliberate intent to foment a "political riot"—it was not a "police riot" or a legitimate dissent, as the Walker Report so glibly contends. Moreover, the response of all political officials in America to the growing anarchy and violence in the decade of the 1960s clearly demonstrates that such officials, in both political parties, are seeking to straddle the principles of the counterrevolution of 1933 and the 1776 Revolution. It is my judgment that official confusion, incompetence, and even moral cowardice in the face of brute force are traceable to this profound contradiction: the 1776 Revolution was premised on individual freedom and choice, and the counterrevolution of 1933 holds, implicitly or explicitly, the philosophy of force and compulsion.

This, therefore, is the context in which I have tried to place the events of Chicago: it is a tragic example of the battleground our nation can become if America's intellectual, political, and moral leaders continue to misread the causes for the violence and anarchy we are now experiencing.

Unlike other works that deal with negative subjects and problems such as the use of violence for political purposes, this work attempts to provide an alternative, positive view of "affirmative America." A general outline of the cause of America's greatness as a nation is embodied in a set of principles—"Finishing the Work of The Founders: An Age of Reform and Repeal." It is an attempt to set forth a redefinition of American patriotism, as opposed to what might be termed "traditional gunpowder patriotism" (that is, the over-emphasis on America's military past and its traditions). It also tries to set forth, in a generalized way, a portrait of the principles that produced the most productive and free civilization in the history of mankind in less than two hundred years. Only by understanding the *true* American tradition can men of reason mount a consistent, articulate, and courageous campaign to effectively oppose future Chicagos and save what, as a nation, we are now fast losing: liberty, law, and the philosophy of reason. For in reality it was this tradition that was under attack in Chicago in August 1968.

This work is not written for the intellectual, communications, or political communities that sought either to fix the blame for Chicago on Mayor Daley or to excuse away the violence and disruption as the work of "children." It is one person's report to the American people, who are neither sick, corrupt, nor indifferent, but, unfortunately, just confused because of the treason and betrayal by the intellectual, moral, and political leadership of the verities of freedom, rights, and reason.

The week of street warfare in Chicago in August 1968 was a stern warning to America and to the world. Now let me explain why.

Jeffrey St. John
New York City
March 6, 1969

"The most candid of revelations . . . have been dismissed as 'going off the deep end' by the very people who, for their own sakes, had the best of all reasons for listening with careful attention. . . ."

Hermann Rauschning
The Revolution of Nihilism
1939

COUNTDOWN
TO CHAOS

I

What the Whole World Was Watching

"THE WHOLE WORLD IS WATCHING, THE WHOLE WORLD IS WATCHING," the crowd in front of the Chicago Hilton Hotel chanted, as police and demonstrators violently clashed in a scene that would be seen across the nation, and eventually the world. It was a little before 8:00 P.M. on Wednesday, August 28, 1968, in Chicago at the height of the Democratic Convention. What the crowd was referring to in its chant was the fact that national TV network cameras, mounted on the marquee of the Hilton Hotel, were to record the "confrontation" between the Chicago police and the demonstrators. Ostensibly, the demonstration by some violent radicals and revolutionaries, and idealistic youth, was to protest what they believed was an immoral war and the convention of a political party that made that war possible.

But what was it the whole world was watching? To answer that question fully, one needs to know the events that occurred long before the Democratic Convention even convened. Was the violence that erupted in Chicago during the last week in August "spontaneous rage" against the alleged inflexibility of our political institutions, such as the Democratic Convention? Or, was it a premeditated assault on the American political process? If the conclusion is that this was premeditated violence, in which many innocents became pawns, one must also conclude that it was a violent attack on the freedom of the entire political system, and on the individual American who secures from that system certain rights and liberty.

As to the issue of whether the Chicago Convention disorders were premeditated, this is not a moot point. Clear and irrefutable evidence was in possession of this author and his associate, William Good, weeks before. In fact, our findings that a minority of radicals and revolutionaries would seek to stage-manage what later turned out to be a "political riot" were published in the August 19, 1968, issue of *Barron's*. And we detailed what was planned for the week of the Democratic Convention. We warned in "Ballots or Bullets?" that:

... a carefully organized civil disturbance of major (perhaps unprecedented) proportions will be touched off by a handful of self-styled American Marxists. . . .

There is every indication that the white radicals now heading for Chicago hope their scheme of disruption will ignite widespread rioting, looting, and sniping on a scale dwarfing that of recent incidents in Cleveland— [July 1968] or Miami.

If all this comes as a rude shock, it shouldn't. The intentions and goals of domestic Marxist revolutionaries have been well documented. (In *Barron's*, for example, by Alice Widener and other writers.) *The problem is that such warnings largely have been ignored by government and the communications media. . . .* On the unofficial agenda at Chicago, therefore, may be the *first brutal attempt by American radicals to force political decisions through mob violence or the threat of it—the beginning of a new phase in America's revolutionary war of the 'Sixties.* [My emphasis.]

This is a crucial point: violence was deliberately used to try to force political decisions. In the verbal warfare that later erupted between Democratic Party regulars, dissident delegates, and those who sought to excuse the initiators of violence, this point was totally ignored.

An important corollary point has been largely ignored since the early days of the U.S. civil rights movement: revolutionary leaders have consistently used masses of demonstrators to stage "confrontations" with the police aimed at provoking violence against themselves—so as later to claim "police brutality" (which they had purposely helped provoke). This technique of "confrontation" had been successfully employed by the radical student movement on numerous university campuses after the civil rights movement merged with the college student protests. At Chicago this technique of "confrontation" was employed with great success.

However, after the major "confrontation" in front of the Hilton Hotel, the misreading of the meaning of what the whole world was watching was compounded by political leaders, members of the press and mass media, and certain intellectuals who share certain basic philosophical and political premises with the initiators of violence in the streets. One such premise and goal was the takeover or destruction of the Democratic Party by its radical elements. But more important, the conflict inside and outside the convention was a struggle between two groups contending for power: the regular liberal and conservative elements in the party, and the more radical members who were determined to rule or ruin.

Liberalism Loose in the Streets

It should not have surprised anyone familiar with the American political scene to find many members of the press, mass media, political, and intellectual communities generally defined as "Liberal" seeking to excuse away or shield from the public view what, in fact, the whole world was watching during Convention week. What happened in Chicago was Liberalism loose in the streets; the participants in the street violence were not the uneducated, the poor, or white or black criminals, but middle class and upper-class young people who had been or were being educated in some of the finest Liberal institutions of learning in the nation. This was true whether they were McCarthy supporters, Yippies, New Left radicals, or simply college youth in search of excitement. Underlying the apologies or excuses for the actions of those inside and outside the convention was the need of members of the Liberal press, political, and intellectual communities to evade this reality—that these were the children of Liberalism, with all its pretensions to progress, peace, and justice.

The cause for this contradiction is not as difficult to understand as it may first appear. For one lesson Liberalism failed to teach—a lesson all free men and nations must never forget—is that *no individual or group of individuals has a moral right to initiate physical force or the threat of force to achieve its objectives.*

Since the early 1960s, and even before, Liberal professors, members of the press, politicians, and intellectuals had explicitly or implicitly taught the children of Liberalism that it was morally proper, in the fight for Negro "equality" and civil rights, to use such force or the threat of force. Civil rights "demonstrations," allegedly peaceful, became less so and moved from scattered violence to continued clashes with police in "confrontations" until they ceased to be a cause for civil rights alone, and became a front for more extreme forms of radical political activity. This can be seen in the merger, after the assassination of John F. Kennedy, of the student-based civil rights movement into a predominantly radical movement—and later, in the merger of black, student, peace, and anti-war groups into the united front that showed up in Chicago.

Liberalism made all this possible, not only by its preachments, but by its active encouragement of street action without recognition of the consequences of such a policy of action. Also ignored was the precedent set on the basis of which other groups with real or contrived grievances also took to the streets. In the years before Chicago 1968, Liberals had consistently claimed that the growing series of city and campus riots were the product of poverty, discrimination, or alienation.

In Chicago, however, the conspicuous absence of poor blacks and the participation of the educated "children of Liberalism" was in itself an ominous event despite almost five years of civil unrest and violence. The educated in the streets, the so-called leadership of tomorrow, were taking to their extreme end the major premises of the Liberal philosophy: the belief that as ordained agents of future history it is proper to force individuals to act against their will.

Not all Liberals evaded or blinded themselves to the ugly and sinister implications of the drama in the streets during the Democratic Convention. On the contrary, Liberal NAACP Executive Director Roy Wilkins was blunt and to the point when viewing the violence in Chicago. Observing that no blacks played a significant or leading role in the Convention disorders, he wrote that the "dirty work" that went on was "guerrilla insurrection":

> The error in Chicago was that the police used not restraint but night-stick repression. If in the excitement they stepped over the line, it must be said that the provocation came first. . . .
> The U.S. must always yield to change, but not to guerrilla insurrection. That was what was attempted at Chicago and was abetted, in confusion, by many who are not insurrectionists. It is not a blanket endorsement of the excesses of the Chicago police to point out that when a deadly rattle is heard the listener is on notice to defend himself.[1]

What is most disturbing about the nature of that "deadly

---

[1] Roy Wilkins, in a syndicated column reprinted in *U.S. News & World Report* (September 23, 1968).

rattle" is that it was reminiscent in some ways of what took place in both pre-Soviet Russia and pre-Nazi Germany in the earlier part of this century.

Russia and the Weimar Republic Revisited

The amazing similarity of the street violence in Chicago to what took place in Russia prior to 1917 and in Germany prior to Hitler's complete takeover in 1933 is not difficult to trace. For example, one of the major leading philosophers of the New Left, seventy-year-old West Coast university professor Herbert Marcuse, is fully familiar with the politics of polarization by street violence. A German-born Marxist, Marcuse in his own student days was a street brawler and agitator with the Socialist Spartacist Movement. Student radical admirers of Marcuse applied such historical lessons in confrontations at the University of California at Berkeley, San Francisco State University, Columbia, and at the Chicago Convention.

These "confrontations" are not for the purpose of settling disputes or resolving grievances; such "purposes" are mere front issues. The real intent of those who initiate violence and street agitation is to perpetuate a continuing civil crisis as a means of weakening the social fabric of society, softening it up for its future takeover. This was precisely the technique employed in pre-Soviet Russia and pre-Nazi Germany.

Those who were in the streets of Chicago knew full well this technique and how successful it had been in the past. For example, the Students for a Democratic Society, headquartered in Chicago and very active in the Convention's week of disorders, uses as its point of reference the ill-fated Russian Revolution of 1905. Columnist and magazine publisher Mrs. Alice Widener, writing prior to the disorders at Columbia and Chicago, observed:

> An over-all theme of SDS today is that 1968 can be "the 1905" of the *American revolution*. What the radical students mean is that they know they cannot *bring down the American government as soon as 1968*, but they expect that their violent revolutionary activities, even though put down this year, *will force the police to use force against students and thus create resentment against our government* in the same manner as the unsuccessful Marxist-inspired Russian revolution of 1905 did against the Czarist regime.[2] [My emphasis.]

---

[2] "Ten Days in April," *Barron's* (March 1, 1968).

A year after the abortive 1905 Russian revolution, French anarchist Georges Sorel published his classic work, *Reflections on Violence*—a working blueprint of continued street violence as a weapon to weaken and, ultimately, bring down a social order.

Many Liberals recognize the ominous import of the politics of confrontation, and even the more leftist intellectuals have come to realize the dangers it poses—particularly in view of the nightmares created in Europe prior to both World Wars. Irving Howe, editor of the Socialist-inclined *Dissent* magazine, wrote that the Chicago disorders were frighteningly reminiscent of what the German Communists employed just after World War I. In fact, Howe notes, Lenin himself became so concerned over the German Communists' use of street violence (called the theory of electrification) that he persistently admonished its practitioners. It was believed by those who practiced the art of street turmoil and violence that this was the way to "electrify the masses" into a state of revolutionary fervor. Instead, Howe points out, it did just the opposite by antagonizing the German middle class, the workers, and other groups until the populace grew weary and united behind any political leader who promised to restore law and order. Adolph Hitler made such a pledge in his climb to power. Howe then notes:

> It would be an exaggeration to say that the Communist tactics caused the rise of Hitlerism, but no exaggeration at all to say that they helped the Nazis come to power. . . .
>
> The advocates of "confrontation" seem undisturbed by the fact that *they are setting precedents which could lead to a major crisis for democracy*. If it is permissible for opponents of the war to burn Government records, why may not neo-Fascists do the same thing a few years later? If it is permissible for left-wing students to seize buildings in behalf of virtuous ends, why may not their action *become a precedent for doing the same thing in behalf of detestable ends?*[3] [My emphasis.]

The New Left hopes that by setting such precedents it will create and foment a major crisis in the American political

---

[3] "The New 'Confrontation Politics' Is a Dangerous Game," *The New York Times Magazine* (October 20, 1968).

process. Their concern is not the American political process which they consider hopelessly corrupt and beyond redemption (or unworkable for their intents); their concern is revolutionary warfare.

American Liberalism Under Attack

While Liberalism was wild in the streets, it was under violent attack from those who had been raised and educated in that tradition. It was a case of the pupil turning on the teacher. Liberal intellectual and labor leader Gus Tyler contended that the target of the "provos" (as he termed the street agitators) was "the core of American Liberalism" and that "the idea is to wipe out the middle ground as in pre-Hitler Germany." Furthermore, Tyler contends the radicals inside and outside the convention were "reaching out for control of the party, with Vietnam as the major issue." He then warned:

> If the battle at the Democratic Convention was a scene out of the Theater of the Absurd, foreshadowing *the possible fate of the national Democratic Party in the years ahead* ... then the battle in the streets was an even more revealing omen of the coming conflicts in America between the "provos" and the police, between the kids and the cops. *It was a miniature preview of the nation's fate should the polarization of politics proceed in the U.S.* . . . . [My emphasis.]

> The most sophisticated in the streets were the members of the Students for a Democratic Society (SDS) and their assorted allies, who had come to Chicago for a *confrontation.* They chose the Democratic Convention to wed praxis—to use an old-fashioned Leninist word—to theory. The theory called for polarizing politics by provoking police power. The praxis was to apply the theory to the symbol of the world Establishment: the Democratic Party of the U.S.A. The end result was a howling success for the new revolutionaries.[4]

A Brick Through the Storefront of Freedom

True to the goal of the revolutionaries to create a continuing state of crisis, the violence at the Democratic Convention was only one of the countless incidents of growing anarchy and violence in the nation's cities and college

---

[4] "The Liberal Crisis—Now," *The New Leader* (October 7, 1968).

campuses. In the twelve months of 1968 there had been riots, the assassinations of Martin Luther King, Jr., and Senator Robert F. Kennedy, threats on the lives of political leaders, sniper attacks on policemen across the nation, and a wave of arson, bombing, and burning of various defense or related institutions. Chicago was but a continuation of the crisis, incited or caused by deliberate revolutionary acts which date back to the first eruption of riots in New York's Harlem in 1964 and, in the fall of that same year, the surfacing of student unrest at the University of California at Berkeley.

America in 1968 seemed to be history repeating itself. Indeed, the same philosophy which underlay the actions of the street agitators in Weimar Germany in the 1920s and early 1930s was manifest in many who went to Chicago to keep alive the crisis of fear that was progressively gripping the nation.

What the whole world was watching, then, in the week of street warfare in Chicago, was the brick of violent revolution being defiantly thrown through the storefront of individual and political freedom. The tragedy is that while Chicago was a warning of worse things to come, millions of Americans were misled or confused as to who threw the brick, why, and for what end.

II

The New Politics: The Matrix of Mob Revolution

"We intend to take the party," announced Clarence Jones, a Negro alternate delegate from New York to the Democratic Convention. "In four years those people sitting in the convention will be relics. The party belongs to the people, as the streets belong to the people."[5]

Jones was one of at least five hundred dissident Democratic delegates and alternates who had stormed from Convention Hall and converged on Chicago's Grant Park in a sympathy protest march for those radicals, McCarthy workers and supporters, and other assorted individuals who had clashed with the police earlier in the evening of Wednesday, August 28, in front of Chicago's Hilton Hotel. It was this violent "confrontation" which millions of Americans had seen on television and in news photos, and which many millions more around the world had seen by relay television. What the world watched was the culmination of almost three years of radical leftist activity and organization to form a political movement in America for the express purpose of either seizing and destroying the Democratic Party, or forcing from power the Democratic Party regulars, and in the process driving the Party farther to the extreme left.

Julian Bond, the Affable Revolutionary

Standing with Jones and other dissident delegates and alternates in the early hours of Thursday morning, August 29, was Georgia's Negro legislator, Julian Bond. He is the bright, handsome, articulate former press chief for the southern-based Student Nonviolent Coordinating Committee. SNCC has abandoned marches and demonstrations in favor of Black Power militancy and, in some cases, violent guerrilla warfare. Earlier during Convention week Bond had been

---

[5] *Rights in Conflict,* The Walker Report to the National Commission on the Causes and Prevention of Violence (New York; Bantam Books, December, 1968), pp. 335-336.

placed in nomination for Vice President, but was later withdrawn since he was just twenty-eight years old and thus inelegible. But this event provided Bond extensive exposure on national television, and the press featured him in almost all its stories on the Chicago Convention, so he was not an unknown when he marched off to Grant Park.

Julian Bond must have felt a sense of great satisfaction, personally as well as politically. A few years ago he and Stokely Carmichael and other white radicals in America had helped to organize the National Conference for New Politics (NCNP). Three summers later, here was Bond beguiling the gullible press with his image of affable sincerity and willingness to work within the Democratic Party. Work he did, knowing full well that his friend and fellow radical, Tom Hayden, one of the founders of the Students for a Democratic Society, had been out in the Chicago streets helping to pave the way for the attempted seizure of the Democratic Party after the Vice President's defeat. As Reese Cleghorn wrote in a flattering piece on Bond in the New York *Times* following the convention:

> Many people see Bond as one of the rallying figures in a rebuilding of the Democratic Party. To bring it out of the shadow of the New Deal and make it conform with the new forces emerging in the country. . . .
> Bond has known and worked with some who led the action [outside the convention hall], such as Thomas Hayden. He does not speak against them. But he seems to start from some of the same premises and to come out in a different place.[6]

It has not been spelled out by Bond and other members of the New Politics what is meant by bringing the Democratic Party "out of the shadow of the New Deal." But the actions of the dissident delegates inside the Convention, and the radicals and their allies outside, hardly encourage one to believe that it will be anything but an attempt to take the party further to the left and *beyond* Franklin Roosevelt to greater government control of the economic, social, and political sector.

---

[6] "Quiet, But Angry Rebel," *The New York Times Magazine* (October 20, 1968).

Twenty Years Before—The Legacy of the Left

As the violence spilled over into the streets of Chicago, it was forgotten that twenty years before in the same city a similar radical leftist move for political power had been launched—the Progressive Party headed by Henry Wallace, Roosevelt's former Vice President and Secretary of Agriculture. Like Senator Eugene McCarthy of Minnesota in 1968, Wallace was no Communist, but he allowed himself to be put in the position of drawing support from Communists and non-Communist radical leftist individuals and organizations. As was Wallace's campaign, Senator McCarthy's campaign was centered on the issue of U.S. foreign policy and its opposition to Communist aggression. The newspaper, *Guardian* (that first came to life during Wallace's campaign when it was called *The National Guardian*), editorialized on the McCarthy campaign three weeks before the Convention:

> . . . the McCarthy campaign, while nothing like our conception of what is necessary, is the political manifestation of years of protest activity—primarily by blacks and students. . . .[7]

Unlike 1948, however, the leadership of the radical Left was not about to delude itself into thinking that a third or fourth party campaign could ever hope to succeed. Henry Wallace and his Progressive Party in 1948 polled a mere 1.57 million votes out of 49 million cast. In 1968, the aim of the radical Left and its allies was to wreck or to seize control of the Democratic Party from the Vietnam "hawks" and later transform the party into an image more conducive to its New Politics image.

Henry Wallace's defeat in 1948 did not discourage the extreme Left and its Communist allies from the hope of eventually coming to power via the political process. However, in the Eisenhower years between 1952 and 1960 the Left almost went into total eclipse. It was not until the advent of John F. Kennedy's New Frontier in 1961 that the Old Left began to promote itself as the New Left; first, via the civil rights movement and later, through the student protest movement on college campuses. After the assassination of President Kennedy in November 1963 and the 1964 re-election of Presi-

---

[7]SDS Strategy: Organizing in Chicago," *Guardian* (August 3, 1968).

dent Johnson, the radical leftists saw their opportunity to
mold a political coalition of blacks, students, and anti-war
groups into a single political hammer for striking a blow
against free political institutions and against America itself.

The New Politics—Blueprint for Brute Force

The first active attempt to form a coalition of radical
political groups, made up of students, blacks, and anti-war or
peace groups, occurred in August 1965. A meeting was held
at the leftist Center for the Study of Democratic Institutions,
at Santa Barbara, California. Present at this first meeting were
Julian Bond, Stokely Carmichael, and other black and white
radicals.[8] Later, in November of 1965, a second meeting was
held, and out of this meeting the name National Conference
for New Politics emerged. Some of the early participants,
supporters, and organizers of NCNP would later engage in the
street violence outside the Convention or in the disruptive
activities inside the Convention as delegates or alternates. The
New York *Times* reported in December 1965 that an NCNP
policy statement disclosed that, "The first steps have been
taken toward the formation of a political movement that
would link civil rights, various student protests, and opposition to the Vietnam war."[9]

This linkup was for the express purpose of forging an iron
fist of political action, utilizing the various campus and urban
riots as a weapon to weaken the Johnson administration and
to pressure it to compromise a successful prosecution of the
Vietnam war. All the urban and campus riots between 1965
and 1968 must be seen as a weapon for the political purpose
of forcing Johnson not to run—at the same time causing the
defeat of anyone who was unwilling to take an appeasement
view of what the Communists were trying to achieve with
their "wars of liberation" in Vietnam and Southeast Asia.

The NCNP had as one of its principal allies the Chicago-
based Committee for Independent Political Action. CIPA was
headed by Negro comedian Dick Gregory, who was very
much in evidence during the Chicago Convention disorders.

Another radical leader in Chicago during the Convention
was Rennie Davis who, along with Gregory and other radi-

---

[8] "New Political Force Rising Across the U.S.," Houston *Post* (August 7,
1966)
[9] The New York *Times* (December 9, 1965).

cals, signed a CIPA-produced statement in December 1965 that read in part:

> It is now time to get a truly independent and anti-establishment political movement going. The under-signed feel that it is time to make the voice of independents felt at the ballot box. . . .[10]

An all-day organizing CIPA conference in Chicago on January 15, 1966, was attended by a cross-section of radical black and white groups, including Communists, SNCC, and SDS. New York *Times* reporter James Corry revealed that the goal of the meeting was "to coordinate civil rights demonstrations and Vietnam protests and to challenge the political machine of Mayor Daley [of Chicago]."[11]

Also present at this January 1966 meeting was another Chicago '68 organizer, David Dellinger, who had worked with Gregory, Davis, Hayden, and others in what was known as the Vietnam Day Committee. CIPA later merged with NCNP after Gregory had unsuccessfully run for Mayor of Chicago in the fall of 1966. However, NCNP attempts at political activity were not so much for the purpose of winning but for organizing unsuspecting and idealistic individuals. As reporter Paul White of the Houston *Post* wrote seven months after the CIPA 1966 meeting:

> While Democrats and Republicans worry over Vietnam and party unity, a vast number of left-wing activists, civil rights militants, peace insurgents, and Stevenson liberals have established a united front aimed at the Washington adminstration and altering "the American way of life." . . . In less than a year the NCNP has become a rallying point for pacifists, campus radicals, left-wing crusaders, social theorists, and Reform Democrats.[12]

Among the supporters or sponsors serving on various committees of NCNP were the revolutionary Marxist New Left philosopher, Herbert Marcuse, and New York delegate to the 1968 Convention, Paul O'Dwyer. In fact, NCNP in the 1966

---

[10] *U.S.A. Magazine* (January 7-21, 1966).
[11] *The New York Times Magazine* (January 23, 1966).
[12] Houston *Post* (August 7, 1966).

elections ran candidates in California, New York, Mississippi, and Alabama, and helped with either NCNP manpower or money. It was these same states that became the center for dissident delegates on the floor of the 1968 Democratic Convention. As Julian Bond wrote in a 1966 NCNP fund appeal letter:

> We are encouraged to find that many peace and civil rights candidates who made strong showings in their first bids for office are now seeking to build viable grass roots organizations in their districts to continue effectively the challenge in November and in 1968. NCNP has created a committee on 1968 to explore methods of keeping peace and social energies alive after the 1966 election.[13]

Fueling the Fires of Protest

Taken as a whole, the radical college campus activity on behalf of peace and the anti-Vietnam protests in 1966, 1967, and 1968 had two express purposes. One was to pressure Johnson to trim his policy over the war, while fueling the fires of radical protest along the path leading toward Chicago in August 1968 and beyond. The riots and unrest served the added purpose of keeping the nation in a state of crisis and agitation. The political activity of the NCNP and the marches, like the April 1967 Vietnam Week organized by David Dellinger, only added to and multiplied this growing sense of crisis in the country.

It was this background that most Americans were not permitted to view and which the Walker Report, a study of the violence at Chicago during Convention week, never touched on. The Walker Report tended to believe that the background for Chicago extended only to the Pentagon march of October 1967—which was true, in part, since almost all the organizations at the Pentagon also went to Chicago. However, it failed to point up the importance of the radical political movement which goes back to 1965 and the National Conference for New Politics convention in September 1967.

Fortunately for the nation and for Chicago, a breach had been created between black and white militants at the NCNP 1967 convention. As a result, Chicago lacked the cohesive element necessary to become a major disaster area that would have made Watts, Newark, and Detroit look like campfires in comparison.

---

[13] Quoted in *U.S.A. Magazine* (September 2, 1966).

III
Why the Blacks Backed Out of Chicago

During the weeks preceding the convention, Rennie Davis, the Chicago coordinator for National Mobilization [Committee—organizing the radical protests at the convention] had been in contact with the Blackstone Rangers, a South Side gang of black youths. Davis tried to negotiate an agreement with the Blackstone Rangers to protect political peace workers from a racial clash in the ghetto. The deal never materialized. Blackstone Ranger people were also contacted by Abbie Hoffman [hippie Yippie leader] and encouraged to join the Festival of Life [a Yippie rally] in Lincoln Park. Very few blacks, as it turned out, appeared in Lincoln Park during convention week. . . .[14]

Political leaders, members of the press, and commentators were mystified as to why black militants had not joined in the troublemaking in Chicago. Their absence at the Convention is no mystery; the answer lies in a break that took place between the black and white radicals at the National Conference for New Politics convention in Chicago shortly after the riots in Newark and Detroit in the summer of 1967.

Blacks as the Battering Ram of Revolution
Ever since the early 1960s white radicals and revolutionaries have looked on Negro ghetto life in America as the social nitro needed to fuse an explosion for violent revolution. During the summer of 1967, black militants at a Black Power conference in Newark, New Jersey, took steps that would alter what the radical New Left publication, the *Guardian*, called "the black movement . . . [as] the cutting edge of our movement." Black leaders began to feel used by white radicals and, from their view, all the payment black people were getting was gutted and burned out ghettos and rioters being shot or killed by "white racist honkey cops." The resentment of black militants and revolutionaries was first fueled by the drive for separation between white and black radicals. This

---

[14] *Rights in Conflict, op. cit.,* pp. 56.

break in the summer of 1967 was to manifest itself not only at the National Conference for New Politics convention in August 1967, but also at the Pentagon March in October of the same year, in the crisis at Columbia in April 1968, and in Chicago at the Democratic Convention.

Blacks were no longer to be taken for granted as the battering ram for white-directed, Marxist-inspired revolution. If anything, the black revolutionaries were going to do the leading and whites would do the following. This first became abundantly clear at the August 1967 NCNP-sponsored "The New Politics Convention on 1968 and Beyond."

When Blacks Boycotted Whites

The NCNP convention, August 31 to September 4, 1967, was held with high hopes of some 127 Communist, radical, revolutionary, peace, and liberal groups from twenty-seven states, the District of Columbia, and Puerto Rico. Many had converged in the hope of deciding whether to run a separate "peace ticket"—headed, hopefully, by Dr. Martin Luther King, Jr., who spoke at the NCNP convention, and Dr. Benjamin Spock. However, the NCNP convention quickly demonstrated that it was hardly headed for a harmonious meeting.

Blacks boycotted the meetings and formed their own "Black Caucus." Their major demand was voting representation far out of proportion to their numbers. Vowing to boycott the convention with a total walkout, the blacks put the whites into a panic and they capitulated. The convention was then badly split, contributing to the chaos that ensued for the five days of meetings.

Just as serious was a black resolution condemning Israel for its "Zionist imperialism" in the June 1967 Arab-Israeli war. This forced a further fissure between the blacks and whites, particularly among those Jewish delegates who supported Israel and had raised money for the NCNP convention. Blacks contended that the resolution did not imply anti-Semitic sentiments, but nonetheless it did contribute to the rupture between the delegates and, in the process, splintered a coalition that had been taking shape since the Watts riots of 1965.

Rennie Davis' attempt to include in the Chicago disorders gangs like the Chicago Blackstone Rangers was a desperate effort to provide the radicals in Chicago with "shock troops." But the blacks made it clear at the NCNP convention that they were no longer willing to receive the blunt end of police "confrontations." What may have greatly contributed to the feeling that whites were using blacks as revolutionary "cannon fodder" was the joy which permeated the convention in the wake of the 1967 Newark and Detroit riots. As Socialist Washington Henry reported after the NCNP meeting:

> Most of the people at the convention seemed positively happy at the ghetto violence which has resulted in the death of many Negroes, and acted gloriously vindicated by the trigger-happy response of Guardsmen and police. They applauded joyfully at every reference to violence. . . .[15]

Two Blows at Black Mob Action

After the breakup of the NCNP convention in disorder and confusion, the first indication that the blacks meant business came during the October 21, 1967, March on the Pentagon. Repeatedly, the white radicals and revolutionaries tried to induce Negro leaders in predominantly black Washington, D.C., to participate in the march and to ignite riots in the capital's worst Negro slum areas. Officials were so convinced that the radicals meant to ignite riots that during the Pentagon March large concentrations of Federal troops were massed in the area adjacent to the worst Negro slums. The radicals' idea was to ignite riots in the city slums in order to draw troops away from the Pentagon so that the "forces of peace" could rush the building and score a massive propaganda victory—they had momentarily stopped the Pentagon "war machine." The plan fizzled.

Six months later the worst rioting in the nation took place in Washington, D.C. It was led by the blacks, doing their own thing and leading their own "rebellion" without white support or direction, after the assassination of Martin Luther King, Jr.

The second failure to trigger ghetto riots coordinated by white-led demonstrations was during the April 1968 disturbances that hit New York's Columbia University. Black students kicked out white radicals from one of the occupied buildings at Columbia and set up their own "liberation area." It was no coincidence that many black militants refused to go along with the white radicals' plan to stage a confrontation at Columbia in the hope that the disorders would spread to the

---

[15] "The New Politics Box," *Dissent* (November-December 1967).

surrounding Harlem community. This is why the "front issue" of the university's gym construction, with its racial over-
tones of allegedly "encroaching on Harlem" was so important
to the SDS radicals.

Columbia's administration was not oblivious to the attempts to spread the conflict beyond the campus. Nor were
some Negro leaders. As former New York chairman of the
Congress of Racial Equality, Clarence Funnye, later wrote:

> . . . the issue which sparked a $50-million riot in New-
> ark was not unlike [Columbia's] own present situation.
> Substitute Newark and Newark Medical College for New
> York and Columbia . . . and throw in an igniting device
> (arrest of a cab driver in Newark and arrest of black stu-
> dents in New York) and there you have it.[16]

SDS founder Tom Hayden's presence at Columbia was for
the express purpose of achieving what he and other white
radicals, in concert with black militants, had achieved in the
July 1967 Newark "rebellions": violence.

Hoodlum "Headhunters" at Chicago

When Rennie Davis had failed to secure the cooperation of
the Blackstone Rangers and other Negro militants in Chicago
to act as "shock troops" and street agitators, the radicals
turned to a white motorcycle gang called the Headhunters.
This development was disclosed when an undercover agent
for Cook County (City of Chicago) Attorney's Office infiltrated the group known as the Yippies. Robert Pierson stated
in his testimony before the House Committee on Internal
Security in October 1968 that:

> The gang which [he] infiltrated provided "muscle"
> for the Youth International Party [Yippies] and other
> groups intent on disrupting Chicago during the con-
> vention. . . . In return for providing protection for the
> Yippies, the motorcycle gang was provided with girls
> and dope.[17]

Pierson also revealed that five hundred sticks of dynamite
had been stored in a south-side Chicago garage, 10136 Indi-
ana Avenue, for use against the police; the dynamite had
been stolen by the Headhunters in Ohio in early August.
Moreover, Pierson revealed that Rubin was "bitter" about the

[16] "While Harlem Slept," *Village Voice* (May 9, 1968).
[17] "Bares Yippie's Bombing Plot," Chicago *Tribune* (October 4, 1968).

fact that the massive show of police and National Guardsmen in Chicago "had discouraged thousands of followers from coming to the city."[18] In his conversations Rubin told Pierson beforehand:

> ... that the street fights of the night before [at the Hilton Hotel] would occur. He also allegedly said that the demonstrators "should isolate one or two policemen and then kill them. ... We should keep the disorders going till we take over the government, just like in Russia."[19]

That Rubin's intentions, such as the use of explosives and killing of police, did not completely materialize does not diminish the danger posed by him and other dedicated revolutionaries. For Rubin, Hayden, Hoffman, and others have clearly spelled out the long-range goal of their game of confrontation. Rubin, closely linked with the Peking-oriented Progressive Labor Movement, stated in November 1967 shortly after his participation in the Pentagon March:

> The goal? A massive white revolutionary youth movement which, working parallel in cooperation with rebellions in the black communities, could seriously disrupt this country, and thus a breakdown would be an internal catalyst for a breakdown of America's ability to fight guerrillas overseas. Thus defeated abroad by peasant revolutionaries, and disrupted from within by blacks and whites, the empire of the United States will find itself faced with rebellions from fifteen different directions.[20]

Mirror of the Nonmonolithic Mob

The chaos at the NCNP convention and the refusal of radical blacks to be drawn into the disorders of the Pentagon, Columbia, and Chicago, illustrate the degree of disagreement and internal dissension that exists within the ranks of the New Left revolutionaries, be they black or white. It has been this nonmonolithic nature of the New Left that has confounded Government and law enforcement officials in developing a sophisticated strategy to deal with the "politics of confrontation." This official failure has provided the New Left a number of successes by default.

Throughout history, revolutions have been made by a mere

---

[18] *Ibid.*
[19] "Yippies Wanted Control of the Country," Baltimore *Sun* (October 4, 1968). (AP dispatch from Washington, D.C., October 3, 1968.)
[20] "Lighting the Fuse," *Village Voice* (November 16, 1967).

minority. The upward mobility of such a movement is dependent on official confusion, if not on the actual incompetence of those who fail to understand that front issues, like civil rights, university reform, and Vietnam, are the weapons of revolutionaries. These issues are used to enlist idealistic supporters who later may be "radicalized" through emotional propaganda appeals—thus coming to accept the tactics and goals of the revolutionaries. To have treated the groups that converged on Chicago as a monolithic group was a mistake on the part of the city of Chicago. To underestimate the extreme difficulty of sorting out the revolutionaries from the idealistic is also a mistake.

To come to grips with the problem, officials and police must have a better working knowledge of how revolutionaries operate. A sophisticated study of past revolutionary movements is required, along with a clear portrait of America's revolutionaries—many of whom were in Chicago during Convention week. Chicago demonstrates the danger the revolutionaries pose and offers some sound lessons for the future. As Liberal and labor leader Gus Tyler points out:

> The real danger for the future . . . is not what happened in Chicago but failure to learn the lesson of Chicago—to recognize that the provos, by themselves, add up to merely a frenzied few. They have only one great skill: the ability to initiate negative actions based on mass emotions and the mass movements of others. *The good Kennedy and McCarthy and anti-war kids were just cannon fodder for the anarcho-intellectuals.*[21] [My emphasis.]

---

[21] "The Liberal Crisis—Now," *The New Leader* (October 7, 1968).

IV
The Pentagon and Yippie Politics:
Prelude to Chicago

The Pentagon siege can be treated as a tactical event to be analyzed and criticized as one possible model for future physical confrontations. This is a necessary process; there will be more occasions for physical confrontations and they ought to be much better planned than the Pentagon was. Can we do better at the Democratic National Convention in Chicago?[22]

The October 21, 1967, March on the Pentagon in Washington, D.C., was not only a prelude to Chicago but a crucial turning point in the American anti-war movement. David Dellinger, co-project director of the Pentagon March and an editor of *Liberation*, stated at an October 23 press conference that "marches" were out and "resistance" was in. In other words, overt violence was to replace covert violence. Although the same individuals and groups at the Pentagon were also to show up later in Chicago, the contrast in how officials handled the Pentagon March and how they handled the events during Convention week was remarkable. At the Pentagon, officials mousetrapped the marchers; in Chicago, it was the other way around.

The Revolutionary Fists That Failed
In a strategic sense the Pentagon March was a failure, if not a fiasco, whereas Chicago was a triumph for the radicals and revolutionaries. David Dellinger's comment in *Liberation* that future marches should be better organized was a tacit admission that the October March in Washington had not gone as planned. First, no ghetto riots were triggered as the marchers had hoped. Second, officials were ready and waiting for the demonstrators when they descended on Washington. Allen Woode, a New Left sympathizer who was on active duty with the military at the Pentagon during the March, contended later that:

Everyone who came to Washington walked smack

---

[22] *Liberation* (November, 1967).

into a Pentagon trap. . . . Objectively speaking, perhaps the best thing that could have happened on October 21 would have been for *somebody to have been killed. For American soldiers to have shot unarmed American civilians exercising their right of free speech would have been a blow from which the administration could never recover.* Yet almost totally, the Pentagon either prevented violence or convincingly argued that the fault was the protestors'.

The Pentagon not only knew what moves were being planned against it; it also demonstrated consummate virtuosity in handling both the protection of the building and manipulation of the news.[23] [My emphasis.]

In Chicago, both the city and the national Democratic Party regulars could have drawn heavily on the experience of officials at the Pentagon as a model for handling the mobs who came to disrupt the city and the Convention. Whether the Pentagon engaged in manipulation of the news is a moot question. Columnist James Reston, on the scene during the Pentagon disorders, provided what is perhaps the best summary of what the October 21 March was all about. In fact, what Reston said about the Pentagon could easily apply to what later happened in Chicago. Reston wrote:

Like many other political "common fronts" of the past, this one contained groups that were determined to use violence and did. The only thing that the groups had in common was that they did not like the war. . . .

But there were also individuals and organizations . . . [who] *want a revolution of American society—and not in the direction of fuller democracy.* In a sense they like the war because it gives them a chance not to simply protest and agitate but to get support from a lot of decent people, including idealistic youngsters. . . .

These groups—all the far left—were the principal troublemakers. . . . If they didn't all lead the civil disobedience they encouraged others to get in the front lines where their heads could be cracked.[24] [My emphasis.]

The Deepening Red of the Radicals

Weeks before the Pentagon March it was clear that the "old" and "new" Communists were hoping to gain from the

[23] "How the Pentagon Stopped Worrying and Learned to Love Peace Marchers," *Ramparts*, (February, 1968).
[24] "The Peace Protest: Everyone a Loser." The New York *Times* (October 23, 1967).

social and political turmoil that members of the peace and anti-war movements had been creating ever since 1964. At the National Conference for New Politics convention in Chicago in September 1967, calls went out for some 200,000 "marching feet" to descend on the Pentagon. (Roughly 60,000 showed up.) The Communists were well represented at the NCNP convention; earlier the party had put out a call for its key members to attend for the purpose of working to gain important positions within the conference.[25] Among those who put in an appearance was the party's chief theoretician, Herbert Aptheker, and from across the country, Dorothy Ray Healey, official of the Southern California Communist Party.

During the heated debate at the NCNP convention about whether to run a fourth-party candidate for the presidential election (this was before Senator Eugene McCarthy announced his intention to enter the primaries), the Communists supported a black militant boycott when their demands for 50 percent of the vote were not met. An observer at the NCNP convention later wrote:

> The Communists mainly sought from the convention a commitment to a third-party race in 1968 which could give them their first opportunity since the 1948 Progressive Party debacle to break out of political isolation.[26]

Although the fourth-party ticket was voted down at the NCNP convention, the black militants ran a presidential candidate, as did the Communists.

Later at the Pentagon, security officials were kept busy photographing the dozens of known Communists and activists who showed up. The March organizers insisted that their actions were not with the intent of aiding and abetting the North Vietnamese, but the official Hanoi news agency, on October 17, announced the formation of a Committee for Solidarity with the American People and wished the Pentagon March "brilliant success."[27]

In the aftermath of the March, House Democratic Leader Carl Albert of Oklahoma charged in a speech that active, hard-core Communist participation was a fact and could not

---

[25] New York *Daily News* (August 29, 1967).
[26] Walter Goodman, "When Black Power Runs the New Left," *The New York Times Magazine* (September 24, 1967).
[27] *Congressional Record*, S17817, (December 4, 1967).

be brushed aside. Further, Republican Minority Leader Gerald Ford of Michigan contended that in an early November 1967 Congressional briefing, President Johnson read a detailed intelligence summary to Congressional leaders outlining the extent of Communist participation in the Pentagon March and said that many were principal troublemakers.[28]

In a press conference prior to the March, then Secretary of State Dean Rusk stated that the White House knew of the extensive and intended Communist participation in the Pentagon March, but did not make an issue of it lest it be accused of smear tactics.[29]

"Smear tactics" or not, there is a voluminous amount of evidence that from the time of the National Conference for New Politics convention in late August 1967 to the Chicago disorders of August 1968, the Communists not only actively participated in events such as the Pentagon March—but were actively involved in the planning sessions for the disorders at the Democratic Convention. And, as co-project directors of the Pentagon March, David Dellinger (who has admitted being a "non-Moscow Communist") and Jerry Rubin had the final sanction of what groups could or couldn't take part in the March—and both are associated with the Peking-oriented Progressive Labor Movement.

However, plus being a prelude to Chicago and a "turning point" in the open employment of violence, a new dimension was added to the Pentagon protests: the emergence of the hippie in New Left politics.

Revolution by Press Preview

In the Pentagon March, hippies, for the first time, became actively *politically* involved. They were so successful in attracting press coverage that a few months after the October affair Jerry Rubin, Abbie Hoffman, and Paul Krassner, who is publisher of a New York underground magazine, sought to make their inclusion a permanent part of the New Left protest movement.

Abbie Hoffman, who was present at the Pentagon, admits in his book, *Revolution for the Hell of It* (a four-letter word descriptive report of his own participation in Chicago), that the Yippies, as the political hippies were called, were a fraud

---

[28] *U.S. News & World Report* (December 4, 1967).
[29] *Time* (October 27, 1967).

fed to a gullible and sensation-seeking press as a serious political movement. The Youth International Party, Yippie, was the figment of the fertile imagination of Rubin, Hoffman, and Krassner. Both Rubin and Hoffman knew that if the area of social conflict were to spread, it would require more participants; the obvious next step was to bring in those drop-outs from society, the hippies. The success of hippies at the Pentagon convinced Rubin and Hoffman that a bizarre life style bottomed on irrational premises and blended with street politics, presented to the media as a serious political movement, would attract the type of attention all three Yippie leaders were seeking. The mass media took the bait in one bite.

A few weeks after Pentagon March, Jerry Rubin spelled out the "new life style" expected of those who intended to descend on Chicago:

> So see you next August in Chicago at the Democratic National Convention. Bring pot, fake delegate cards, smoke bombs, costumes, blood to throw and all kinds of interesting props. *Also football helmets.*[30] [My emphasis.]

This was the first of many succeeding indications that the New Left and the newly formed Yippies meant to disrupt the Democratic Convention. In March 1968 at New York City's Grand Central Station, a violent clash between three thousand hippies, or Yippies, and New York City police previewed what the country could expect at the Convention. The March 22 demonstration was allegedly for the purpose of "welcoming spring." However, Krassner, Rubin, and Hoffman acknowledged that the Grand Central Station clash was "a preview of what Chicago is going to look like at the Democratic National Convention in August."[31]

The following day all three flew off to Chicago to assist in planning the activities for disrupting the Convention. The meeting was held at Lake Villa in northern Illinois and was also attended by David Dellinger, Tom Hayden, and Rennie Davis. The Grand Central "Yip-In" in which many innocent hippies got their heads busted, proved to be an accurate forecast of the Convention week. A national news magazine reported:

---

[30] "Lighting the Fuse," *Village Voice* (November 16, 1967).
[31] "Yippies Will Taunt Democrats in Chicago," *Human Events* (April 6, 1968).

> The Yippies are really pointing toward Chicago. . . .
> Looking back on the melee at Grand Central, many non-
> Yipping hippies are wondering if the politics of YIP are
> not already too controversial for comfort. The Chicago
> shindig, they fear, could well result in a far larger num-
> ber of clubbed and lacerated heads.[32]

The suggestion that football helmets be among the items
for the Chicago "props" was not for offensive purposes, but
for self-protection—as the more experienced protestors had
learned at the Pentagon confrontation. Apparently, the
"spontaneity" of the Grand Central "Yip-In" made the appearance of football helmets less desirable.

Fusion of Divergent Forces

The assault on the Democratic Convention came from
many groups. The tactical lessons learned at the Pentagon, at
the Grand Central "Yip-In," at Columbia, and the various
urban riots were intended to fuse together as a revolutionary
fist to be used against the American political process. The
success of the radicals and revolutionaries, without the help
of blacks, demonstrated more the weakness on the part of
officials than the strength of the street agitators. How would
Chicago have turned out if, as had been the plan, "ghetto
uprisings" had coincided with the demonstrations in downtown Chicago?

This question was not even asked after the disorders. Nor
were the possibilities discussed that the Chicago disorders
served the purposes of the North Vietnamese delegation to
the Paris peace talks and, at the same time, helped divert
world public attention away from the Russian invasion of
Czechoslovakia during the Convention.

---

[32] "The Politics of YIP," *Time* (April 5, 1968).

V

Prague and Paris . . . The Politics of Propaganda

The Communist Party and other "Communist front" organizations *had representatives at almost all Mobilization meetings* but none of them had much direct influence during either the planning period or the convention week insofar as Mobilization's program was concerned. The Progressive Labor Party [Peking-oriented group] was also present, but it, too, played a small role.[33] [My emphasis.]

The Mobilization Committee to End the War in Vietnam held more than two dozen meetings between its first skeleton meeting in December 1967 and its final strategy sessions in the days prior to the Convention. One wonders why the Communists wasted their time attending so many conferences if, as the Walker Report claims, they didn't have much influence during the planning of the disorders in Chicago! In fact, the Communists did have influence, and there is a clear indication that the Chicago disorders were staged, in part, with the Paris peace talks and the propaganda value the violence might create in mind. For example, various Mobilization leaders made trips to Paris only weeks prior to the Convention.

The Trips of the Troublemakers

Perhaps no charge has generated more resentment from the New Left than that they are controlled or influenced by the Communist regimes of Moscow, Hanoi, Peking, and Havana. However, prior to and after every major U.S. civil disorder since the Berkeley rebellion in September 1964, major radical troublemakers have made trips to Communist countries. What they did or said on these trips is not known, but a series of such trips hardly helps the New Left's case in disclaiming Communist influence and pales their own countercharges against their critics for engaging in "smear" tactics and "Red baiting."

For example, prior to Jerry Rubin's participation in the Berkeley disorders of late 1964 and early 1965, he and others

---

[33] *Rights in Conflict, op. cit.,* Summary, p. 33.

made a trip to Castro's Cuba. Tom Hayden returned from Hanoi shortly before the Newark riots burst forth in July 1967. David Dellinger, prior to leading the Pentagon March in October 1967, was in Bratislava, Czechoslovakia. And after the Pentagon March, Hayden was summoned to Cambodia by the North Vietnamese to receive three captured America servicemen; dealing with a radical member of the U.S. peace movement instead of with the U.S. Government decidedly had propaganda advantage for the Viet Cong. The principal troublemaker at Columbia University, Mark Rudd, spent three weeks in Cuba in February 1968, prior to the April disorders (of which Hayden was also very much a part).

David Dellinger returned from Paris and a meeting with the NLF (National Liberation Front) in May 1968 and announced that the Mobilization Committee was going ahead with plans for the Chicago demonstrations. Up until that time it was uncertain, publicly at least, whether the Mobilization Committee would go to Chicago.[34]

In the investigation of the Chicago disorders by a Congressional Committee (in October of 1968), a lesser known Mobilization leader, Robert Greenblatt, freely testified that in June, two months before the convention, he had been in Paris, Prague, and Hanoi—allegedly to try to bring an end to the war. Greenblatt further admitted that while in Paris he met with a Viet Cong representative, a Colonel Lao, and delivered a letter to him from Tom Hayden, who during July 1968 spent two weeks in Paris talking with the Communist Viet Cong.[35]

Jack Newfield, of the pro-New Left New York publication *The Village Voice,* talked with Hayden upon his return, one month before the Chicago Convention, and noted:

> Tom Hayden came home from Paris, where he had spent ten sleepless days talking to the North Vietnamese and American negotiators. . . . He was one of the first Americans to flaunt the State Department's travel ban. He visited Hanoi in December of 1965. Since then he has visited Czechoslovakia, Cuba, Paris, and Hanoi again—all without a valid passport. . . .
>
> Hayden has returned from Paris in a revolutionary mood, what his friend Andrew Kopkind calls "an NLF high" [National Liberation Front].

---

[34] The New York *Times,* (August 18, 1968).
[35] Richmond *Times Dispatch* (October 4, 1968). (AP Dispatch)

Hayden's most recent trip to Paris grew out of the fact that the *National Mobilization Committee had received a cablegram on July 1, [1968] from the North Vietnamese in Paris requesting that either Hayden or Dellinger fly to Paris immediately.* Hayden arrived on July 3 and spent almost two weeks talking to the North Vietnamese. [36] [My emphasis.]

The Paris and Prague Propaganda Ploy

While the aim of the radicals and revolutionaries was to disrupt the Convention and at the same time invite violence on themselves and their idealistic McCarthy supporters (who would in the process become "radicalized"), a dispute broke out between the hard-line Communists and the New Left radicals. It was reported that the Communists feared that violence in Chicago would "adversely affect Sen. Eugene McCarthy's chances at Chicago. . . ."

But the New Left, according to [an] intelligence report, wanted to rampage in the streets and force a confrontation with the police. The repercussions around the world, they argued, would demonstrate the strength of peace forces and help North Vietnamese negotiations in Paris. This was exactly what happened.

This was the reason the State Department issued a warning to the North Vietnamese delegates in Paris to stay out of American politics and get on with the talks. [37]

Such a report gains considerable credibility by the fact that Dellinger, Hayden, and Greenblatt in May, June, and July 1968 had extensive conferences with the North Vietnamese delegation in Paris and with officials in Hanoi.

However, looking back on the Soviet invasion of Czechoslovakia which occurred the week of the Convention, there is considerable reason to suspect that the Soviets held off sending their armies into Prague until the Convention and the violence were well underway. It would not have been the first time that Moscow used the American political process to its advantage. And, in fact, what was happening in Prague was swept off the front pages of the world press by the disorders in Chicago. The White House knew twenty days before the Czech invasion that Moscow was planning such a move. Columnists Drew Pearson and Jack Anderson later wrote that:

---

[36] "Saigon Will Fall in the Dry Season," *Village Voice* (July 18, 1968).
[37] Drew Pearson, Chicago *Daily News,* quoted in *Congressional Record,* H8260 (September 4, 1968).

Those hard-nose agitators—avowed "pacifists" all—curiously have found nothing to protest in the Soviet invasion of Czechoslovakia. Their hero, Ho Chi Minh, actually approved the occupation of Czechoslovakia by Russian tanks and troops.

Indeed, one intelligence report suggests that Communist-liners deliberately provoked the violence in Chicago in an attempt to divert world attention from the Russian invasion. Significantly some of the demonstrators in Chicago waved the same red flags that the Soviet invaders carried into Czechoslovakia.[38]

The MOB Begins to Meet

After the Pentagon March, but long before the invasion of Prague, the Paris peace talks, and the trips of the Chicago troublemakers to Paris, Prague, and Hanoi, the Mobilization Committee to End the War in Vietnam—nicknamed the MOB—began a series of meetings to map plans for Chicago. The first such meeting was held in New York City on December 18, 1967, and attended by roughly seventy people—so the Walker Report states. At a second meeting in the same city, on January 26, 1968, Tom Hayden and other members of the MOB met with several lawyers from the suspected Communist-dominated National Lawyers Guild, which sponsored the meeting. Hayden told the gathering:

> We should have people who can fight the police, people who are willing to get arrested. No question that there will be a lot of arrests. My thinking is not to leave the initiative to the police.[39]

However, at a later meeting Hayden demonstrated his ability to toy with the truth. Hayden and Chicago MOB coordinator Rennie Davis changed their tactics at a March 22-24 meeting attended by Yippie leaders fresh from the Grand Central Station disorders, and major MOB leaders, among others. As the New York *Times* described, it was a meeting attended by "delegates who represented groups ranging from Women's Strike for Peace to the Communist Party."[40] In attendance, too, were black militants and assorted Black Power groups representing the so-called Black Liberation Front.

---

[38] Drew Pearson and Jack Anderson, New York *Post* (September 11, 1968).
[39] *Rights in Conflict, op. cit.*, p. 30.
[40] The New York *Times* (March 24, 1968).

In an effort to induce the blacks to join the Chicago protest both Hayden and Davis pledged:

> The campaign should not plan violence and disruption against the Democratic National Convention; it should be legal and non-violent.[41]

The meeting proved to be a complete failure since the blacks refused to have any part of Chicago. MOB plans were further complicated by President Johnson stepping down on March 31—thereby depriving the radicals of a major "establishment" symbol at which to aim.

Nevertheless, "practice" protests were being carried out as preludes to Chicago in an effort to "radicalize" and mobilize a sufficient number of young people to engage in the Chicago Convention disorders. Hayden was helping to stir up trouble at New York's Columbia University in late April, and Rennie Davis and three thousand "peace protestors" became involved in an April 27 clash with police in Chicago. Writing in the aftermath of Columbia, in which he called for "two, three Columbias," Hayden spelled out the basic premise to be employed in Chicago.

> A crisis is foreseeable that would be too massive for the police to handle. It can happen. . . . What is certain is that we are moving toward power—the power to stop the machine if it cannot serve humane ends.[42]

To achieve this crisis, however, the members of MOB needed to manipulate a situation where the police would be provoked into brutal action. And even before Hayden made his pledge to disrupt and destroy, the Students for a Democratic Society (SDS) publication, *New Left Notes*, realistically assessed "non-violence":

> To envision non-violent demonstrations at the convention is to indulge in unpleasant fantising [sic]. It should be clear to anyone who has been following developments in Chicago that a non-violent demonstration would be impossible.[43]

To further illustrate the duplicity of Hayden, Dellinger, and other radical leaders, we need only consult Hayden's testimony before the House Internal Security Committee

---

[41] *Rights in Conflict, op. cit.,* p. 27.
[42] "Two, Three Columbias," *Ramparts* (July, 1968).
[43] *New Left Notes* (March 4, 1968).

two months after Chicago. The New York *Times* reported:

> Mr. Hayden testified that the demonstrators never had any intention of promoting or provoking violence.
>
> Mr. Hayden said the purpose of the organizers was to "bring the rank and file of the Democratic party— decent, respectable, middle-class people—to Chicago" to protest the war in Vietnam and to demonstrate racial and student unrest.[44]

McCarthy, Kennedy, and the MOB

McCarthy's strong showing in the spring primaries of 1968 and Robert F. Kennedy's entrance into the Presidential race greatly complicated matters for MOB members. The New Left movement, in general, had suffered because of McCarthy and Kennedy; each drained potential recruits for the radical ranks into their respective campaigns. The murder of Senator Kennedy solved this problem for the MOB. With Kennedy out of the way, it became obvious that Hubert Humphrey would win the nomination—that McCarthy did not have a chance. The MOB leaders, while unhappy at the loss of potential recruits, had sought to use young McCarthy supporters as front-line "cannon fodder." But the growing certainty that McCarthy would not be the Democratic nominee worked to the greater advantage of the radicals; disappointed McCarthy supporters turned to disruptive tactics as an expression of their disappointment. In other words, they became "radicalized."

In a late June 1968 conference, MOB leader Rennie Davis announced that plans would proceed for protests at the Convention. He qualified his earlier pledge that they would be "non-violent" with the statement:

> But a lot depends on how we are treated. If we are unable to get public space for our meetings or sufficient housing, and if we are Maced and arrested by the Chicago police, we can't be held responsible for what happens.[45]

And in New York, Tom Hayden echoed the Davis theme in a press conference that announced that some one hundred organizations would go to Chicago; almost all had been involved in the October 1967 Pentagon March. Hayden stated:

---

[44] The New York *Times* (December 2, 1968).
[45] "New Left Revives Plans for Convention Protests," The New York *Times* (June 26, 1968).

We are planning tactics of prolonged direct action to put heat on the government and its political party. Several demonstrations are planned. We realize that it won't be a picnic, but responsibility for any violence that develops lies with the authorities, not the demonstrators.[46]

[46] The *Guardian* (July 6, 1968), excerpts of Hayden's press conference at New York Fifth Avenue Peace Parade Committee's headquarters.

VI

Provoking the Police "Pigs" — Warfare Against Freedom

Among the dissidents planning to come in protest were violent revolutionaries, pro-Peking sympathizers, Communists, anarchists, militant extremists, as well as pacifists, poor people campaigners, civil rights workers, and moderate left-wingers.[47]

It is curious that the Walker Report concludes that "those committed to such actions [of disruption] appear to have been unable to combine a broadly based following nor a well-organized plan."[48] Evidence in the body of the Walker Report suggests that however loosely affiliated, the groups who went to Chicago to cause trouble had both a broad-based following and an organized plan. Even more strange is the Report's comment that both the underground and regular press, in the weeks before the Convention, published provocative radical statements, plans of action, and threats of terrorism that could not, in the Report's words, "be responsibly dismissed." While many of the threats and plans of the radicals proved unfounded or unfeasible, the general outlines of what eventually happened were clearly spelled out beforehand.

Duplicity of Dellinger, Davis & Co.

Members of the MOB, in a series of meetings with the city officials on August 2, 5, 10, and 13, carried off the pretense of seeking permits to hold demonstrations. During these meetings, an impasse between the city and the MOB leaders developed which has never been fully clarified. The city did not, as MOB leaders later insisted, deny them parade permits. The impasse developed over the *route* of the proposed march. Davis, Dellinger, and others insisted that the parade permit allow the protestors within "eye shot of the Convention." The city of Chicago had suggested a number of alternate march routes, none within "eye shot of the Convention," knowing full well that to grant their request would invite an attempt on the part of the radicals to physically rush the Convention hall.

---

[47] *Rights in Conflict, op. cit.*, p. 17.
[48] *Ibid.*, p. 18.

Rennie Davis is quoted by the UPI on August 13 as saying that "storming the Convention itself is not out of question." Hayden, a week later, contended that it was "ridiculous" for the city to fear that "a group of people in shirtsleeves could pose a threat to a hall protected by thousands of armed policemen, Federal agents, and National Guardsmen."[49]

But it was not a successful storming of the Convention hall the MOB leaders wanted. They knew that a rush would be repelled by National Guardsmen and police—an event television film crews and reporters would be certain to record. The "garrison police state" would thus be shown repelling, brutally perhaps, the "people" from exercising their right of dissent in front of a barbed wire Convention site. As Hayden himself wrote before going to Chicago:

> We do not welcome the beating or killing of even a single member of our movement. . . . But we know that serious struggle cannot begin without each individual preparing to accept jail or suffering as the price.[50]

Prevented from gaining a parade permit within "eye shot" of the hall, the MOB leaders hypocritically went ahead and filed a legal suit to compel the city to grant them a parade permit—contending that the city had ruled out *any* march. It was a bold lie. As to the insistence of the MOB leaders that their members sleep in the park, the city offered the use of the Edgewater Beach Hotel, closed because of financial troubles. This offer was rejected and the MOB leaders insisted they would urge their members to "sleep in the park" with or without a permit.

Dellinger's dishonesty is further exhibited when he said that if Mayor Daley had been "easier on us, we would have been more aggressive."[51] SDS national secretary Michael Klonsky, also in Chicago, later stated that "if [Daley had given] us the park, we would have gone to the streets."[52]

MOB's Secret Meetings

While Dellinger, Davis & Co. were piously carrying on in public, two not-so-public meetings were held. The first, held on

---

[49] "War Foes Reject Offer From Daley," The New York *Times* (August 22, 1968).

[50] *The Rat* (August 23—September 5, 1968).

[51] Ethel Romm, "Blueprint for Revolution," *New York Magazine* (October 14, 1968).

[52] *Ibid.*

August 4 at the Chicago Highland Park Hotel, was attended by forty-eight persons, including ten known Communists. The meeting was chaired by Dellinger and it was disclosed that "press releases" were prepared—*three weeks before the Convention*—about victims of "police brutality."[53]

The MOB public relations chief also announced at the meeting that "statements had been prepared for delegates to the Convention which were favorable to NMC [National Mobilization Committee]."[54] And Rennie Davis announced that requests would be made to the U.S. Department of Justice to investigate the police!

At the second secret MOB meeting, held at 1012 Noble Street in Chicago on August 18, the group was told that

> . . . if no permit was issued to march on the Amphitheater [Convention hall] "we will attempt to close down the loop." Plans also were made at the meeting to prevent organizers of the disorders from being arrested.

Hayden asserted that "if the city doesn't meet our demands, it will be war in the streets and it should be.[55]

As Convention week drew near, MOB medical teams, part of the New Left Medical Committee on Human Rights and the Student Health Organization, began arriving and setting up first aid stations. These actions were hardly calculated to convince city officials that MOB's protests would be non-violent. Nor did the city's distrust of the MOB diminish with scenes of radicals working out in Chicago's Lincoln Park, practicing karate kicks to the groin, chops to the head, and "snake dances." A snake dance is a technique perfected by leftist Japanese student street brawlers to break up police charges by linking arms and holding on to each other's waist or belt, forming a tight wall of human bodies. Well-trained demonstrators employing such a tactic can move in any direction. This effect resembles a snake dance.

But there were more ominous signs of calculated assault. As Convention week opened, the Walker Report found that on Saturday, August 24:

> There were reports from police undercover agents that persons in the park had purchased *oven cleaner and*

---

[53] Ronald Koziol, Chicago *Tribune*, quoted in *Congressional Record*, E7710 (September 5, 1968).
[54] *Ibid.*
[55] *Ibid.*, E7711.

ammonia to be used as weapons against the police....
Upon hearing these reports individual policemen naturally became apprehensive. Matters were not helped
when the Yippies released a pig in the park and one of
them yelled: *"kill the blue-shirted pigs and release hu-
mans, mother f--kers."*[56] [My emphasis.]

On that same day, Davis coolly proclaimed for the national
press:

> There is no question we're faced with a conspiracy to
> prevent our demonstrations.... I think we're already
> faced with a police state here in Chicago, and it's now a
> question whether the Constitution will be completely
> suspended here in order to prevent expression of all
> dissent during the convention.[57]

And Dellinger echoed his associate's remarks in a separate
news report:

> If Daley wants a confrontation, I'm afraid he'll have
> it. We are ready to go to jail and hospitals to protest our
> rights.[58]

"The Chicago Cops Are Soft"

A reading of all the pertinent material compiled on the scattered acts of violence on Saturday and Sunday, August 25 and
26, clearly indicates that provocative language and taunts di-
rected toward the police were calculated to force the police to
lose their composure. Obscene references about the wives of
the policemen undoubtedly contributed to individual breakdown of police discipline, resulting in scattered incidents during this two-day period. The final clash came when demonstrators defied an order to clear the park after curfew on Sunday
evening and the police attempted to enforce this order. One
should think that the order to clear the park would apply
equally to all who had remained, with innocent viewers and
"observers" not excluded; this is how the police understood
the order. In the inevitable confusion some nonrevolutionary
bystanders and newsmen were clubbed, Maced, and/or arrested. The situation conformed perfectly with what Hayden
had anticipated prior to the Convention:

> Consider the dilemma facing those administrating the

---

[56] *Rights in Conflict, op. cit.,* p. 135.
[57] The New York *Times* (August 24, 1968).
[58] New York *Daily News* (August 25, 1968).

aggressive apparatus [the police—Editor] . . . they cannot distinguish "straight" radicals from newspaper men or observers from delegates to the convention. They cannot distinguish rumors about demonstrations from the real thing.[59]

One very real factor in this clash was that the police assumed that anyone in the park after the curfew was up to no good, otherwise why be there; other contributing factors were the widespread area and darkness. (This will be examined in greater detail later.)

The agitation of the police was increased with additional events on Monday. As the Walker Report states:

> At about 5:15 A.M., Monday [August 26], the Federal Bureau of Investigation received reports that demonstrators were planning such harassment tactics as turning on fire hydrants, calling out police and fire department units on false alarms, and stringing wire between trees in Lincoln Park to stop three-wheel police motorcycles.[60]

Throughout Monday scattered clashes took place between police and demonstrators. One ABC newsman, James Burns, complained that he was prevented from filming arrests and that a $900 camera lens had been smashed and his soundmen clubbed. By Monday, however, police were aware that some demonstrators were deliberately staging acts of brutality for newsmen. The Walker Report quotes the U.S. attorney who observed:

> A man was seen sitting on the grass [in Grant Park] with his back against a tree. He had a bandage in his lap and was talking with three men who had camera equipment. He then leaned back, put the bandage to the left side of his forehead and the cameraman began taking pictures. They were asked for their names and for whom they worked and they all scurried off without answering.[61]

The main publicity event of the day, portrayed in numerous photos around the country, was a rally around Logan Statue with the young radicals waving the red and black flags of revolution and anarchy. The clashes between demonstrators and police were carried into the night, part of the action

---

[59] *Ramparts* (August 25, 1968).
[60] *Rights in Conflict, op. cit.*, p. 159.
[61] *Ibid.*, p. 166.

taking the form of fires set in trash baskets, street lights broken, and police cars stoned.

However, the key radical leaders took time out for a meeting early Monday evening of which a secret tape recording was made. According to the Chicago *Tribune* reporter Robert Wiedrich, one radical leader stated:

> These Chicago cops are soft. If that had been New York cops, they'd have busted our heads. It's gonna be easy to take these coppers and this town apart.[62]

"It was this information," the *Tribune* reporter wrote, "that prompted the show of force. . . . It was this information that finally convinced even the most charitable that this was no peaceful group that would pelt Chicago with flowers."[63]

Propaganda: Weapon of Warfare

Convention week was an ugly demonstration of political street warfare, yet little has been said about the psychological climate, augmented by incessant propaganda, that helped create this conflict. For example, it is clear that the New Left openly promoted its plans for disrupting the Convention for two reasons: first, to rally forces sympathetic to its position and to "put out the word"; second, to create a psychological climate of fear and uncertainty in the ranks of the Establishment in the hope that this uncertainty would contribute to rash acts on the part of authority.

The city of Chicago knew very early that the MOB leaders would seek to use the issue of "police brutality" as a propaganda weapon. In no small measure, therefore, the fury of the police against the demonstrators was a product not only of incessant abusive language and taunts, but of the long-standing frustration of policemen over being portrayed in the mass media as mindless brutes. Since 1964, the media have painted the police as the villains in civil rights, peace, and student protests. The uncontrolled fury of the Chicago police and the equal fanaticism of the demonstrators toward the police was the end result of what was, in effect, a propaganda campaign during these years. Seeds of hatred and mistrust had long been sown between the police and the unthinking young people who came to Chicago primed to battle with the "brutal pigs."

---

[62] Chicago *Tribune* (September 4, 1968).
[63] *Ibid.*

One observer said of the demonstrators:

> The thing about this crowd was that since it thrived on confrontation it behaved in a way much different than any other crowd I've ever seen. During racial riots, the police would break up the crowd and the crowd would stay broken up. It might regroup in another place but rarely would it head back for direct confrontation with its assailants.
>
> This was a most unusual crowd. This time . . . the police would break people's heads but the crowd would not run away. What it would do . . . [was] regroup and surge back to the police and yell more epithets, as much as saying *"Do it again."*[64] [My emphasis.]

---

[64] *Rights in Conflict, op. cit.*, pp. 154-155.

VII
Chicago's Political Al Capones on Tuesday and Wednesday

As various credentials fights underway at the Amphitheater were lost by the challengers, the mood of the Grant Park crowd [on Tuesday, August 27] gradually changed. Transistor radios and reports from delegates kept the demonstrators continually apprised of the results of the convention activities. As the crowd grew . . . its mood seemed to harden. . . .

At this point, the crowd grew unruly and began to throw missiles at police. The police, according to one witness, were bombarded by Pepsi Cola cans filled with urine, beer cans filled with sand, ping pong balls with nails driven through them and pieces of ceramic tile. He also says he saw glass ashtrays and plastic bags filled with urine thrown from hotel windows.[65]

(It was later found that most of the missiles falling on the police from the hotel windows came from those rooms occupied by workers for Sen. Eugene McCarthy.)

The violence of Monday escalated on Tuesday and reached a violent climax outside the Hilton Hotel on Wednesday night. While there were a series of marches Tuesday morning and afternoon, the major clash between police and demonstrators did not occur until Wednesday night. Among the radicals who harangued the swelling crowds on Tuesday evening was Yippie New Left leader Jerry Rubin.

Words as Revolutionary Weapons

Black Panther Bobby Seale, one of the few black militants involved in the Chicago disorders, addressed the Grant Park crowd of 1,500, calling for revolution and urging the election of Eldridge Cleaver, Black Panther candidate for President. Seale also told the crowd to get guns, and closed by saying, "If the pigs [meaning the police] treat us unjustly tonight, we'll have to barbecue us some of that pork."[66]

Jerry Rubin followed Seale with a similar call or incitement to violence. Rubin's bodyguard, undercover agent Rob-

---

[65] *Ibid.*, p. 207.
[66] *Ibid.*, p. 187.

ert Pierson, later reported that Rubin kept a detailed diary which stressed four points. 1. Initiate tactics to deliberately provoke the police. 2. Infiltrate the ranks of the McCarthy workers. 3. Block streets and traffic. 4. Initiate mass charges against police lines, armed with caustic oven cleaner, golf balls spiked with nails.[6 7]

These four tactics were carried forward on Tuesday and Wednesday. But the principle weapon used to incite the rioters were the countless speeches of Seale, Rubin, Negro comedian Dick Gregory, and other radical leaders. For example, after various clashes had erupted throughout the evening, a rally to celebrate a Lyndon Johnson "un-birthday party" was held at the Chicago Coliseum, attended by some three thousand people. This legal indoor rally was taking place at the same time that police were being pelted and verbally abused in front of the Hilton Hotel. At the rally, folk and rock singing groups entertained the gathering, followed by a vicious speech by Dick Gregory:

> If there had been a bunch of young people who challenged Hitler the way you challenged Mayor Daley, there might be a whole lot of Jews alive today. Now the world knows what kind of city we have here.
> What you're trying to do to this system is worth getting knocked for and stomped on for. What you're doing to this system is something we old fools should have been doing years ago. I hope you don't turn around. I hope the more tear gas they pour on you, the more determined you are to break this damn system.[6 8]

Other radical speakers rose to deliver denunciations of Daley and the Chicago police. The meeting, described by one observer, was "like a revival meeting." Such is the role words play in whipping up a mob for revolutionary action.

Later some two thousand attendees left the Coliseum after Professor Sidney Peck told the crowd, "They're beating kids in front of the Hilton," which at the time was not true. As the crowd marched from the rally, another crowd, swept out of Lincoln Park by police, headed for Grant Park across from the Hilton Hotel. En route, the Lincoln Park crowd threw trash cans into store windows, set trash cans afire, broke police car windows, and pelted officers with rocks and bottles.

[6 7]Jerry Greene, "Uncover Leftist Plot to Ruin Convention," New York *Daily News* (August 31, 1968).
[6 8]*Rights in Conflict, op. cit.*, p. 208.

From Tuesday midnight to 1:30 A.M. police were taunted and hit with plastic bags filled with human excrement and urine, but no major conflict developed. The primary reason for the absence of greater violence was that the police did not attempt to enforce the park curfew. A few hours later, 3:00 A.M. Wednesday, the National Guard relieved the beleaguered Chicago police.

Thus, despite the efforts of the radicals to whip up the mobs on Tuesday night, they failed because they lacked the basic pretext to trigger violence: police insistence that the curfew be obeyed.

The Warning About Wednesday

On August 9, almost three weeks before the major clash in front of the Hilton Hotel, the Intelligence Division of the City of Chicago reported that:

> Due to talk around the office of the National Mobilization Committee and the general attitude of Rennie Davis and Tom Hayden, the reporting investigator feels that *on the night of 28 August, 1968 there will be widespread trouble* through the efforts of Davis and Hayden.[69] [My emphasis.]

In the face of their Tuesday night failure to precipitate a major conflict, the radicals were even more determined to create a violent confrontation; thus the Wednesday clash confirmed the advance warning provided the police almost three weeks before.

Events started midday with a rally held at the park's bandshell between 1:00 and 4:00 P.M. (The MOB committee obtained a permit for this particular rally, apparently to have a legal rallying point for dispersed forces, and from there activities could be—and were—extended.) The evening before, Dellinger had announced that there would be an attempt to march on the Convention hall on Wednesday, and that became a subject of heated discussion during the afternoon bandshell rally.

Some demonstrators were reluctant to force a march to the Amphitheater, fearing violence. Dellinger and others, intent on creating an incident, favored the proposed march, knowing it would fulfill their plans for precipitating violence.

---

[69] "The Strategy of Confrontation," City of Chicago (September 6, 1968).

So this discussion, in addition to inflamatory speeches, again set the climate for action. Among the speakers were writers William Burroughs, Norman Mailer, and, again, Dick Gregory.

Action began at about 3:30 or 4:00 P.M. when demonstrators tore down an American flag from a pole standing in the park. As one activist started to take the flag down the crowd, numbering some ten thousand and by now well primed with speeches, began chanting "Tear it down." At this action, a few policemen moved in and seized the demonstrator at the flag pole who, by then, had run up what appeared to be the "red flag of revolution."

The response by the police to this act was deeply emotional; they had just seen the national flag defiled and they roughly handled the demonstrator or began clubbing him—a point which is open to dispute.

In reaction, the crowd began yelling, "Pig, pig, kill the pigs." And as if on cue, or waiting for such an incident (response from the police), chunks of concrete, rocks, bottles, clay floor tile, and balloons filled with paint or urine began pelting police. Reinforcements arrived later and a police charge ensued, clubbing and flailing at anyone in the way. Tear gas was used and in the process of this conflict some thirty policemen were injured. No count is available as to how many demonstrators were hurt or hospitalized.

Later the park rally was resumed, followed by David Dellinger's announcement that there would be an attempt to march on the Amphitheater—in direct violation of police and city warnings. But the march, or the attempted march, was the pretext needed to force a clash with the police in front of the Hilton Hotel at a little before 8:00 P.M. Wednesday, August 28—in full view of the network TV cameras and reporters.

While the Whole World Watched

Wrote *Christian Science Monitor* reporter Saville Davis, who was on the edge of the crowd at the Hilton:

> Everyone knew it was coming, and everybody was ready. Above the Hilton marquee were television cameras of CBS and NBC with their festoons of power cables sweeping back into the Hotel and their red eyes unblinking. Out in the middle of no-man's-land was a NBC television truck and ABC mobile units were all around. *The stage was set.* All . . . was recorded at the

perfect distance of 20 to 30 feet by the television camera above us on the marquee. They had an unimpeded vision of the clubbing and manhandling.[70] [My emphasis.]

In the three-plus hours between the afternoon rally and the evening clash, Dellinger and Professor Sidney Peck sought to "negotiate" with city and police officials for a "peaceful" march to the Amphitheater. In reality, however, this was a stalling tactic to enable hard-core organizers to move demonstrators out of the park and to the front of the Hilton. During this brief period the massing of thousands in front of the hotel was accomplished—it should be noted, that *this* was accomplished without any police incidents, or provocations on the part of the demonstrators!

The police were completely taken in by this deception, since it would not have served the leaders of the MOB to have a confrontation with the police in the park—partly because it was growing too dark for adequate film coverage, and because it was too widespread an area. The TV media and the press had assigned personnel to various groups and knew generally where the action would take place. Thus the rioters and media converged in front of the Hilton—and the TV cameras recorded for the world the "repressive police state" measures of the Chicago-Daley machine.

Once they were grouped in front of the Hilton—and cameras—radicals in the center of the crowd began hurling objects at the police and pushing the front ranks of the demonstrators forward. At the same time troublemakers began spitting in the faces of the police officers. The Walker Report states that, in an effort to prevent newsmen and innocent bystanders from being hurt, once the decision had been made to try to clear the area, a deputy superintendent of police asked, "Will any non-demonstrators, anyone not part of this group, any newsmen, please leave the group."[71] As pre-arranged, demonstrators sat down in the street and police asked them to leave the street while those demonstrators with portable loudspeakers continued to yell, "You don't have to go, hell no, don't go."

The Walker Report then relates that:

The crowd was becoming increasingly ugly. The dep-

---

[70] "A Night of Raging Protest," *Christian Science Monitor* (August 30, 1968).
[71] *Rights in Conflict, op. cit.,* p. 249.

uty superintendent states that demonstrators were pushing police lines back, spitting in officers' faces and
pelting them with rocks, bottles, shoes, glasses, and
other objects.[72]

None of these provocative events were discerned by the TV
cameras, network commentators, or glib critics of the police.
But at the same time the breakdown of discipline of the police
themselves and their indiscriminate clubbing of any persons in
the area of conflict contributed to the chaos and multiplied the
impression on TV that the riot the "whole world was watching" was—despite unrelenting and obscene abuse—totally the
fault of the police. As the Walker Report observed:

> There is little doubt that during this whole period . . .
> the preponderance of violence came from the police. It
> was not entirely a one-way battle, however.
> Firecrackers were thrown at police. Trash baskets
> were set on fire and rolled and thrown at them. In one case
> a gun was taken from a policeman by a demonstrator.
> "Some hippies," said a patrolman in his statement,
> "were hit by other hippies who were throwing rocks at
> the police." . . . One of the demonstrators says that
> "people in the park were prying up cobblestones and
> breaking them. One person piled up cobblestones in his
> arms and headed toward the police." Witnesses reported
> that people were throwing "anything they could lay
> their hands on. From the windows of the Hilton and
> Blackstone hotels toilet paper, wet towels, even ashtrays
> came raining down." A police lieutenant states that he
> saw policemen bombarded with "rocks, cherry bombs,
> jars of vaseline, jars of mayonnaise, and pieces of wood
> torn from yellow barricades falling in the street." He,
> too, noticed debris falling from the hotel windows. . . .
> An attorney who was present also told of seeing
> demonstrators kick policemen in the groin.
> In another case, a Chicago police reporter said in his
> statement . . . he heard "hissing sounds from the demon-
> strators as if they were spraying the police." Later he
> found empty lacquer spray and hair spray cans on the
> street. Also he heard policemen cry out, "They're kick-
> ing us with knives in their shoes." Later, he said, he
> found that demonstrators "had actually inserted razor
> blades in their shoes."[73]

---

[72]*Ibid.*, p. 250.
[73]*Ibid.*, pp. 261-262.

In twenty minutes the clash was over. And within hours millions had watched the effectiveness of a few political gangsters. Just as the Chicago gangster "Scarface" Al Capone sought to use force and terror to enforce his demands, so the radical leaders in Chicago operated on the identical principle: muscle as the quickest means to achieve their ends.

Not surprisingly, after the Hilton clash, one of the political gangsters, David Dellinger, announced of an issue that had consumed his energy only a few hours before:

> I see no point in marching to the Amphitheater. It would be a futile move to march to a place where its obscenity has already been revealed.[74]

To many this may have seemed so, but the real obscenity was in the streets where violent force and revolution were revealed in all their naked and terrifying ugliness.

---

[74] New York *Post* (August 29, 1968).

VIII
The Disrupters Inside the Democratic Convention

Wrote *Christian Science Monitor* reporter Saville Davis of the Convention in the wake of the Hilton Hotel clash:

> The vast auditorium was trembling with suppressed excitement and concern. Everywhere delegates and reporters were watching television screens on the battle downtown and no one knew when the volcano would erupt. . . .
> The collision is especially poignant because the earlier ghetto riots, which were more violent physically on both sides, *did not touch the political process* of the country. The Chicago repression, by contrast, and the protest which it routed, were *carried directly into the nomination of a candidate for President of the United States* with the whole nation looking on.[75] [My emphasis.]

As surely as the street thugs in Chicago played their roles in this unprecedented event in American political history, the dissident delegates within the Convention acted out disruption for the same end: that of projecting the image of the United States to the world as a "fascist police state." Most of the hard-core dissident delegates, many of them members of the National Conference for New Politics, were out to rule or ruin the Democratic Party, with Vietnam as the "front issue." They were allies of the street radicals—as evidenced later by their solidarity rally in Lincoln Park—despite their suits, neckties, and pious claims of wanting to "work within the party."

The Disruptive Doves
Long before the street warfare began erupting, the dissident Democratic "doves" made up their minds that the only way to wrest the nomination from Hubert Humphrey was to try to throw the Convention into disorder and chaos. The idea was to initiate credential fights, debates over Vietnam, and other such issues for the purpose, as one McCarthyite put it, of "making Humphrey look bad and hope for the best."[76]

---

[75] *Christian Science Monitor, op. cit.* (August 30, 1968).
[76] *Newsweek* (September 2, 1968).

The major hope of the doves was the fight over the peace plank, but this was dealt an early death blow with the Russian invasion of Czechoslovakia. As James Reston of the New York *Times* commented, "The arguments about the Democratic platform . . . now seem irrelevant." And one of the leading supporters of Senator George McGovern, Ted Sorenson, had to admit that "there's no question it hurts our case."

Columnist and Convention observer Roscoe Drummond noted that disruptive delegates and supporters of Senators McCarthy and McGovern

> . . . seized every opportunity to embarrass and harass the pro-Humphrey majority in part because these *delaying and divisive tactics were all that was left to them.* Their mood became more reckless and rancorous as their strength declined. They harshly complained about how they were being denied their rights by rulings from the platform, but their dominant purpose was to disrupt the proceedings in the hope that the Humphrey forces would disintegrate. In the end the anti-Humphrey forces disintegrated with their fantastic pleas to recess the convention without nominating anybody and transfer it to another city.[77] [My emphasis.]

Their final delaying demand—to transfer the Convention to another city—came correspondingly into play as the delegates watched the clash between the police and their allies in front of the Hilton on Wednesday night.

Hitchhiking on the Hilton Riot

Beset by desperation for an issue, the disruptive dove delegates seized on the police excesses as a last desperate attempt to turn the Convention tide in their direction. The most famous, if not the most outrageous, statement was made by Connecticut Senator Abraham Ribicoff who, in the process of nominating Senator George McGovern, proclaimed that if McGovern were nominated one would not see "gestapo street tactics in the city of Chicago." However, on returning home to seek re-election, Ribicoff found a political time bomb waiting for him; a large segment of voters were angry at his Convention statements. During his campaign, as a consequence, he trimmed his position considerably, almost to the point of condemning the protestors instead of the police.

---

[77]"What the Democrats Did," *Christian Science Monitor* (August 31, 1968).

Ribicoff's Presidential candidate, McGovern, however, piously intoned in the aftermath of the Hilton clash:

> What was going on down on the pavement below was an experience that left me sick at heart. I saw American youth being savagely beaten by policemen simply because they were protesting policies about which they had very little to say.[78]

McGovern had spent much time previous to the Convention articulating positions on behalf of Negroes. Therefore, it is revealing that one of the major civil rights leaders in the nation, Roy Wilkins of the NAACP, was quite blunt as to what the disruptive dove delegates' indignation over the disorders was all about. Stated Wilkins:

> In the convention itself, some individual delegates and parts of certain delegations were tuned in on the Grant Park doings with a view to hooking them to their political objectives on the convention floor. The *Michigan Avenue maneuver* [the Hilton clash] *was a "take-over" operation, not a peace move.*[79] [My emphasis.]

Closed Minds for an Open Convention

The Coalition for an Open Convention (COC) was led by a former president of the National Student Association and a worker for the Southern-based Student Non-violent Coordinating Committee (SNCC), Allard Lowenstein—who was later elected to Congress from Nassau County, New York.

Like Abbie Hoffman and other radicals in the streets outside the convention, Lowenstein and his associates in COC knew well the tactics of massing large numbers of people in a "confrontation" situation for political purposes - much as SNCC had perfected the technique in the South in the early 1960s. Before the idea was scuttled by Senator Eugene McCarthy, who feared violence, Lowenstein was hoping to bring to Chicago upwards of a million supporters and stage a massive rally in Soldiers Field.

The COC group—many from the National Conference for New Politics—presented a preview of the tactics to be employed inside the Convention at a June 28 New York State Committee meeting. The McCarthy "peace wing," led by NCNP member and Convention delegate Paul O'Dwyer, dis-

[78] New York *Post* (August 29, 1968).
[79] Roy Wilkins, *op. cit.* 80

rupted the Committee meeting after a bitter wrangle over delegate seats with the party regulars. After much booing of speakers, three hundred "peace" delegates, including Lowenstein, stormed out of the meeting.[80]

This kind of "putsch politics" was employed during the fight over credentials and the Vietnam peace plank, and later carried to the Convention floor by Lowenstein-led delegates.

The dissident delegates' actions had been anticipated three weeks prior to the Convention by the New Left publication, the *Guardian*:

> Led by Allard Lowenstein, one of the chief architects of McCarthy's campaign, the Coalition [for an Open Convention] will consist of liberals disgruntled with what they feel is a corrupt convention. Whatever the leaders may plan, *it is considered likely that many in the ranks will move to protest and disruption....*[81] [My emphasis.]

The Delegates Go into the Streets

In order to create as much disruption as possible, dissident NCNP delegates fed TV floor reporters false rumors, which many of the networks failed to check out, and took full advantage of the TV cameras and eager reporters. For example, UPI reporter Robert Musel asked:

> Since most other delegates had gone to dinner, would the New York delegation mixed choir have continued singing and swaying as long as they did in the emptying amphitheater if the cameras had stopped?[82]

When all of their disruptive strategems failed, and the peace plank was defeated and Humphrey nominated, the NCNP delegates seized upon the clash at the Hilton Hotel as an issue.

Some five hundred delegates and alternates conducted a "peaceful" march to the Hilton to express their indigation at the "police-state tactics" of Mayor Daley. Holding candles— which had been purchased from a Chicago synogogue by former Kennedy aide Richard Goodwin *before* the Hilton violence—the delegates were greeted by the street guerrillas in the park across from the Hilton with enthusiasm, and someone with a bullhorn exclaimed, "Those candles mark the wake of the Democratic Party."[83]

---

[80] The New York *Times* (June 29, 1968).
[81] "On to Chicago!" *Guardian* (August 3, 1968).
[82] *Congressional Record*, S10319 (September 5, 1968).
[83] *Rights in Conflict, op. cit.*, p. 335.

NCNP delegates like Julian Bond, who had come a long way since the first NCNP meeting in August 1965, and Paul O'Dwyer of New York spoke to the gathering in the park. Clarence Jones, a Negro New York alternate delegate, summed up the feeling of the dissidents when he said:

> I heard you say "Now, not in four years." But don't put us down. We intend to take the party. In four years those people sitting in the convention will be relics. The party belongs to the people, as the streets belong to the people.[84]

The crowd took up the chant. Ellen McCarthy, the Senator's young daughter, also spoke to the assembly:

> I just came down to let you know I'm not going to give up fighting now. I'm with you. Daddy has been watching from the window up there and wanted me to thank you and the delegates here tonight."[85]

That had been late Wednesday night and Thursday dawn. On Thursday afternoon McCarthy addressed delegates and street provocateurs and pledged to work to "seize control of the Democratic Party in 1972."[86]

That evening, delegates, radicals, and McCarthy supporters —some three thousand in all—sought to stage a march to Dick Gregory's house to take up the Negro comedian's offer to have a glass of beer! The march ended in a clash between police and National Guardsmen and the demonstrators. Hundreds were gassed, hit with rifle butts, and arrested— including many delegates after they sought to defy a Guard and police order not to try to march any farther. Thus, in joining the mobs in the streets, the dissident delegates had demonstrated that not only did they share similar premises, but that they were willing to act on those premises even when doing so meant violating law and order by their physical presence and threats of force, or by having force brought upon them. This unity between those in the streets and the dissidents in the Convention hall was overlooked by much of

[84] *Ibid.*, pp. 335-336.
[85] *Ibid.*, p. 336.
[86] *Ibid.*, p. 341.

the mass media. But one publication, thoroughly grounded in the tactics of political warfare, fully recognized the importance of the delegates going down into the streets. As correspondent Mike Davidow of the Communist *Daily World* noted:

> The most significant achievement of the battle of Chicago was that the two struggles on the streets and in the political arena were never before brought so close together. Delegates and demonstrators are returning home profoundly affected by the trial by fire in four of the most hectic days in U.S. political history.[87]

Middle Class Criminals

The violence and disruption that engulfed the Convention set a dangerous precedent in American political life. For the first time threats of force and actual violence were employed in an effort to make political decisions. Those who committed such acts were not the impoverished and uneducated, or of the criminal element. On the contrary, the radical leaders and even the hippies, as well as those McCarthy workers who joined in the violence and vandalism in the Chicago hotels, were young men and women from affluent, middle-class America, with allegedly good educations, and good economic and social advantages. This is also true of those radical students and their sympathizers on the nation's college campuses since the so-called rebellion at Berkeley in 1964. "Middle-class criminal behavior" is the only way to describe what happened in Chicago and what has been happening on the college campuses of the nation since 1964.

These young people are expected to be the leaders of tomorrow. But their use of violence and threats of violence to achieve political ends is an ominous warning for the future of the nation, if they are permitted to persist. After having executed similar tactics in the universities during the four years prior to the Democratic Convention, middle-class criminality was allowed to invade the very political process of the nation —and in its selection for the highest elective office in America. And thus are raised ghosts of the 1920s, as admitted by British journalist Peregrine Worsthorne:

> The frightening fact has to be faced that significant

---

[87] *The Daily World* (New York, August 31, 1968).

organized minorities have despaired of the democratic
process, and make no secret of having put their faith in
revolution. . . . It is what happened in Germany under
the Weimar Republic. Sizeable groups of the German
middle class lost faith in democracy. . . . Despair about
the democratic system became fashionable. Street
violence was allowed to grow, with results that are all
too familiar.[88]

Apparently unmoved by this ominous parallel, a New Left
writer, Don Miller, stated in the *New York Free Press*:

Who knows, one day historians may decide that the
*second American revolution began in Lincoln Park in
Chicago in late August of 1968*, the year the Republicans, Democrats, and Yippies all nominated pigs for
president, and the streets became the only forum for
people to exercise their constitutional rights in. . . .
*Not only did Chicago prove that the street action is
supremely political, it implied that all street action is
political.*[89] [My emphasis.]

---

[88] London *Sunday Telegraph* (September 1, 1968).
[89] "The SDS View," New York *Free Press* (September 5, 1968).

IX
Clean Gene: The Political Pied Piper

I am going to keep the commitment I made, and I pledge that I will stay with the issues as long as I have constituency, and it looks like I still have one. Work within the political system and you can help seize control of the Democratic Party in 1972.[90] [Senator Eugene McCarthy at a Grant Park gathering the day after the major clash between the radicals and police.]

McCarthy addressed the Grant Park throng of supporters, radicals, Yippies, and dissident delegates as "the government in exile," a comment NAACP Executive Director Roy Wilkins later termed "glibness" that ended up as "pure misrepresentation."[91]

However, the role McCarthy played in the disruption, disorders, and violence in Chicago either directly or as a symbol, helped to maintain the climate of unrest. The media, before and since, has been generous in its coverage of McCarthy the Senator and Presidential primary candidate, but woefully neglectful in making a searching appraisal of McCarthy the political animal, and the burden of blame he should share for allowing physical violence to become part and parcel of the American political process. When his stature as a U.S. Senator and primary candidate could have been used to stem the extremism growing in the 1968 campaign, even among his own supporters, he was silent. Thus he shares some of the blame for the violence that reached a climax in Chicago in August 1968.

Holding the Hammer over Humphrey's Head

Weeks, even months, before Chicago, it was clear that supporters of Senator Eugene McCarthy would use the threats of violence, or violence itself, in trying to seize the nomination. A staunch supporter of McCarthy, columnist

---

[90] *Rights in Conflict, op. cit.,* p. 341.
[91] *U.S. News & World Report* (September 23, 1968).

Pete Hamill, sounded the battle cry in late June 1968 when he wrote:

> It must be made clear . . . that young people and the decent people of this country will not stand for Humphrey's nomination. If Humphrey is nominated, the young and decent *will make it impossible for him to campaign*. . . . [Which almost did happen.]
> It must be McCarthy because it can't be Humphrey. If the central committee [the Democratic Convention] gives us Humphrey . . . *we can disrupt, disrupt, disrupt*. Hubert Humphrey simply cannot be handed the Presidency of the United States by a few thousand men. If that happens, then it's really all over for all of us, Baby Blue.[92] [My emphasis.]

A few days after the Hamill piece appeared, the disruption at the June 28 New York State Committee was created by McCarthy delegates. Furthermore, McCarthy's supporters knew the only way they could wrest the nomination from Humphrey was through a combination of disruption and playing to the mass media. As a pro-McCarthy publication, *The New Republic*, phrased it in early July:

> What millions of TV viewers and newspaper readers see and read about national conventions may have an even greater impact in 1968. *That assumption is one on which the McCarthy convention managers are basing their strategy*.[93] [My emphasis.]

It was with this factor in mind that Allard Lowenstein and other McCarthyites sought to stage a massive rally in Chicago with one million supporters as a show of alleged McCarthy strength. McCarthy realized that other more extreme radical groups, like the MOB and the Yippies, were bent on actual violence and on August 12 urged his supporters to stay home and conduct demonstrations in their own communities. But this single, and late, gesture could not contain or stop the forces that McCarthy had earlier helped nurture into existence. And many of the more emotionally committed and enthusiastic McCarthy supporters went on to Chicago. It was

---

[92] "Warning from RFK Camp," *Village Voice* (June 20, 1968).
[93] Paul R. Wieck, "An Open Democratic Convention," *The New Republic* (July 6, 1968).

the more active faction of the McCarthy campaign which either aided or abetted the street rebels or later joined them at the Hilton Hotel confrontation. Columnist William S. White leveled a stern warning when he wrote two weeks before the Convention:

> For the first time in our history there is being raised a clear and present danger, as the president of the American Bar Association has just said in substance, to the most basic of our traditions of free and fair debate and of elementary civility in public controversy.
> The extremists among the backers of the presidential candidacy of Senator Eugene McCarthy are in nearly every instance at the forefront of these disorders. . . .
> Too many of those around McCarthy, if not the Senator himself, are actually finding amusement in the spectacle of shouting and threatening packs who in some instances are almost physically driving the presidential rivals from the stump.[94]

McCarthy Mob at the Hilton

The dissident NCNP delegates and supporters of Senator McCarthy inside the Convention, were in contact with many of the street agitators outside. One bridge between these groups came from among the McCarthy workers, some of them idealistic and well meaning, who were in the hotels of Chicago such as the Hilton. In this regard, the Walker Report observed:

> As the convention week progressed, and their cause did not, many young McCarthy workers had become increasingly sympathetic to the demonstrators outside the Hilton. On Wednesday night they set up emergency first aid rooms on the 15th floor and distributed torn sheets outside the hotel for use as bandages and emergency gas masks. . . . Their support for and collaboration with the protestors were resented by both the hotel officials and the police.[95]

Further, during the Wednesday clash, the Walker Report revealed that both the police and National Guard pinpointed

---

[94]"Gene Must Stop His Extremists," New York *Daily Column* (July 9, 1968).
[95]*Rights in Conflict, op. cit.*, p. 347.

the fifteenth floor as the point from which ashtrays, beer cans filled with urine, and other objects were being thrown at the police. Upon entering the suite after the Hilton security officers had requested it cleared, investigators found fourteen of the fifteen ashtrays missing and some fourteen empty liquor bottles.

Some of the occupants were injured by police in the process of clearing the suite, when they refused to go down to the hotel lobby and, instead, tried to go upstairs to the suite occupied by the Minnesota Senator's aides on the twenty-third floor.

The Senator and his aides cried "police brutality"—ignoring the provocative actions of his supporters—and the Senator sarcastically insisted that because of the police and Guard action "there is some question whether you are as safe in Chicago when you're wearing a McCarthy button as when you don't wear one."[96]

However, a newspaper correspondent, John Edward Fogli, asserted that he personally saw objects thrown from the fifteenth floor McCarthy suite and that when he confronted the Senator:

> I told Senator McCarthy, who denied that any objects were thrown from the hotel, that I had been witness to the same and he interrupted me and stated that "if a few beer cans can't be thrown from a hotel, what is a convention anyway?"[97]

Consequences of McCarthy's Actions

Whether he wished it or not, Senator McCarthy became a front around which the more radical and revolutionary elements in American political life could rally. McCarthy as a candidate was seen by the radicals—and even by the Communists—as a means to an end: political influence to weaken American policy against Communist aggression such as in Vietnam. This is substantiated by comments made at a luncheon at the Terrace Room of the Roosevelt Hotel in New York City on July 9, six weeks before the Convention.

Gathered at the luncheon were assorted radical, pro-Communist, and Liberal "peace" personalities. Mrs. Alice

---

[96] The New York *Times* (August 31, 1968).
[97] *Ibid.*

Widener, a columnist and magazine publisher who has written extensively on the New Left, also attended and she noted:

> According to the cocktail conversation among the more than two hundred guests, the luncheon marked the end of "phase one" of operations conducted by the leftist "in" crowd. The completion of this phase was quietly boasted about with the statement, "We forced the President of the United States to abdicate." A second achievement of phase one was described as "our victory at Columbia" [University].
>
> In cocktail and luncheon conversation, the "in" crowd made it clear they are not the slightest bit interested in who the 1968 presidential candidate will be. They regard Sen. Eugene J. McCarthy as a temporarily useful but expendable tool.[98]

Part of "phase two" was the violence and disruption at the Chicago Convention as a part of trying to "bring down the whole system." McCarthy's actions prior, during, and after the Convention sanctioned the aims of the revolutionaries, particularly in his Grant Park speech after the Hilton violence in which he urged his supporters and revolutionaries alike to "work within the political system and you can help *seize control of the Democratic Party in 1972.*" Whether he was aware of it or not, McCarthy played right into the hands of the revolutionaries, for his words and actions put the stamp of approval on the *aims and goals* of the radicals: the *seizure* of the Democratic Party.

It should be remembered that one aim of the revolutionaries in Chicago was to "radicalize" McCarthy supporters, manipulating them into a situation where violent police action would turn them against the democratic process, the police, and the Government itself. In fact, many of the more militant McCarthy followers planned to join the street gangs if "it becomes clear their man can't win," as New York *Times* reporter Anthony Lukas put it. Lukas interviewed Rennie Davis, Tom Hayden, and SDS national secretary Michael Klonsky six days before the Convention opened. Hayden and Davis admitted that they expected many of the McCarthy supporters who were going to the Convention to participate

---

[98] Alice Widener, "Anti-War Leftists Plan 'Phase Two' of Campaign," *Human Events* (July 27, 1968).

in the "MOB program," meaning a disruptive program with
violence. Klonsky is quoted as saying:

We think lots of them [meaning McCarthy support-
ers] are going to be awfully disillusioned by the time
they leave. We're going to set up forums where we can
talk to them and help them draw the right conclusions
from McCarthy's defeat.[99]

The violence and rioting which Hayden, Davis, Dellinger,
and Klonsky helped precipitate was added insurance that the
McCarthy supporters would draw the "right conclusion."

Resting in the Arms of the Revolution

In the final analysis, however, Senator Eugene McCarthy
emerges from the political year 1968 considerably soiled and
with much revolutionary muck on his hands—whether or not
he was blinded to the fact that his Presidential bid became a
bridgehead for New Left revolutionaries.

He not only raised the false hopes of a great many decent,
idealistic, and dedicated young people, but must be held
morally responsible for allowing his young supporters to be
used as cannon fodder on the front lines of Chicago by cynical revolutionaries and radicals who care neither for democracy, liberty, nor the rights of individuals. They are only
interested in power—the power to destroy the social, political, and economic system in America as we know it today.

One would not be so harsh with Senator McCarthy if it
were not for his performance in Grant Park the day after the
violence in front of the Hilton Hotel. Diana Trilling, the
Liberal author and critic, spelled out the key factor on which
McCarthy failed:

After the hideous police action in Chicago, the liberal
McCarthy, like the liberal Columbia faculty after the
police bust of April 30 [the climax of the 1968 Columbia disorders], was properly outraged. . . . McCarthy
condemned the shocking operation of Daley and the
Chicago police, *but he failed to condemn the New Left
for deliberately designing an action that would provoke
the use of police* and invite excess. And by neglecting to

[99] "Dissenters Focusing on Chicago," The New York *Times* (August 18,
1968).

perform this job of education that was mandatory . . .
[he] bowed in a significant degree to the *view of the
New Left, that any liberalism which means to go forward
with history . . . has no move to make except to dissolve
into the arms of the revolution.*[100] [My emphasis.]

. . . a revolution, it should be added, that wishes to take the
liberalism of the last few decades to its most extreme ends.
For as the radical New Left publication *Guardian* stated after
Chicago 1968:

If our goal is to take power and to replace Capitalism
with a Socialist system, we must start to organize a
movement to accomplish this objective. . . . Ultimately
our goal is a mass movement. We cannot achieve this by
turning our backs to Liberals, to workers. *Today's
liberal—the McCarthy man or woman—must be tomorrow's radical.*[101] [My emphasis.]

---

[100] Diana Trilling, "On the Steps of Low Library," *Commentary*
(November, 1968).
[101] *Guardian* (November 16, 1968).

X
The Mass Media as a Mouthpiece for Mob Rule

"The police undoubtedly overreacted," said David Gins-burg, director of the National Advisory Committee on Civil Disorders (known as the Kerner Commission),

> ... but the [news] media must also bear the burden of guilt in failing to portray the true nature of the organizations and the degree of provocation.
> A balanced picture was not presented to the country. This was true of television and it was as true of the press at the time. This is not to condone the police over-reaction, but it is to say that the country was not told what the police faced.[102]

The American news media, with a few notable exceptions, demonstrated by its coverage of the Chicago disorders that nothing had been learned from the turmoil of the 1960s—the disruptive civil rights movement beginning in the 1960s was nurtured into a national political movement by the help of the news media. The media apparently also learned little after the criticism of its conduct in Dallas in 1963, in the urban riots between 1964 and 1968, and in the student riots of Berkeley, 1964, and Columbia, 1968. To some, the overt bias of the media in its coverage of Chicago was both irritating and puzzling.

The Built-In Bias of the Media

The coverage of Chicago demonstrated once again the commitment of many in the news media to some of the basic causes espoused by those activists inside and outside the Con-vention hall. At least one member of the media confessed, after Chicago, that the American public is deluding itself by believing that television and newspaper reporters can any longer provide balanced reporting of the news.

Jules Witcover, who covered the 1968 Presidential campaign

---

[102] The New York *Times* (September 10, 1968).

for the Newhouse National News Service and who is the author of a book on the campaign of the late Robert Kennedy, contends that the press got a bum rap in Chicago. Why?

> The reader and the television viewer, for years have been fed the notion of pure objectivity as a dogma of the American press; the sophisticated have learned to sort out the routine news story from the interpretative, but others have not, and to them the press has become more and more "slanted." Politicians and bureaucrats at every level have encouraged the public in this latter impression, particularly when they themselves have been under fire by the press, as [Mayor Richard] Daley was.
>
> The new emphasis on interpretation, spurred on by newspapers by competition from televison, has freed newsmen from the narrow confines of the old "objectivity" into areas of analysis once reserved for columnists and commentators. *In a sense it has been a return to what used to be called personal journalism....*[103] [My emphasis.]

His implication, in other words, is clear: Americans by the millions were naive to expect objective reporting of what went on during the Democratic Convention.

"A return to ... personal journalism" may have been very much in evidence in Chicago, but it is a journalism with a built-in bias of many reporters who were educated and reared in the Liberal tradition and thus not part of "middle-America."

The Liberal columnist Joseph Kraft, in the wake of Chicago, pinpointed this factor that contributed to the one-sided portrait Americans received of the events in Chicago. He asked:

> ... do we, as supporters of Mayor Daley and his Chicago police have charged, have a prejudice of our own?
>
> The answer, I think, is that Mayor Daley and his supporters have a point. Most of us in what is called the communications field are not rooted in the great mass of ordinary Americans—in middle America. And the result shows up not merely in occasional episodes such as the Chicago violence, but more importantly in the *systematic bias toward young people, minority groups,*

---

[103] "The Press and Chicago: The Truth Hurt," *Columbia Journalism Review* (Fall, 1968).

and the kind of presidential candidates who appeal to them.[104] [My emphasis.]

Contending that most reporters and commentators come from and represent "upper-income white opinion," Kraft asserts much of the press tends to be sympathetic toward those causes which are in conflict with what the mass of Americans believe or feel. Observes Kraft:

> What this means is that the press is not the public. Between the news media and middle America there is an imperfect relation, a lack of touch, a disharmony. That being so, it seems to me that those of us in media would be wise to exercise a certain caution, a prudent restraint in pressing for plenary indulgence to be in all places at all times as the agents of the sovereign public.[105]

The Explosive Fuse of Such Bias

Some of the fury of the police against many newsmen during Convention week must be viewed as the explosion against a media, rooted in the *non*-middle-America tradition, which has overplayed the civil rights, "peace," and student revolutionary demonstrators, sometimes in the most flattering light, while portraying the police as "brutes." Since the early 1960s the media's bias in favor of protest groups has been less than balanced in presenting the problems faced by the nation's policemen. In some cases they have irresponsibly echoed the fallacious charges of "police brutality" made by such protest groups. The media, too, has been less than diligent in backgrounding its reporters and editors in the nature of violent revolution. In fact, in some cases it has been blinded to the fact that a small minority of Marxist revolutionaries seeks to use issues like peace, Vietnam, civil rights, and university reform as front issues in a systematic campaign to bring America to its knees.

This is what was attempted in Chicago, but few of the news reports from Chicago delved deeply into the motivations of the radicals and, particularly, into their long-range aims and goals. Nor was the build-up of the plans of the revolutionaries touched upon.

As a result, when the press in Chicago took sides, it invited

---

[104] Joseph Kraft, Washington *Post* (September 3, 1968).
[105] *Ibid.*

the explosive fury—inexcusable as it was—of the infuriated police who were spit upon, abused, and physically assaulted. The Walker Report hinted at the frustration of the police, who as a matter of fact belong to middle-America:

> Police emotions were heightened by their impression, as they listened to radio, watched TV and read newspapers, that the media coverage was anti-Chicago, anti-Mayor Daley, and anti-Police.
> There is further support for the police view. On August 30, 1968, a National Guard Colonel was interviewed by NBC in connection with the actions of the Guard and the Police Department in clearing the McCarthy staff suite in the Hilton. The Colonel spoke of the "great job" done by the Police Department. As he walked away he heard one of the technicians and cameramen say to the announcer, *"You can't use that."*[106] [My emphasis.]

A TV Invitation to Violence

> The news media [in Chicago] may be indicted for inciting to violence.
> The mildest parade of young people brings a TV camera crew like a hook-and-ladder truck to a three-alarm fire. Any youngster who will denounce the authorities finds himself surrounded by a ring of extended microphones. *The press has talked so much about violence that it has vested interest in violence. It will look silly if it doesn't get it. This is a case where the "medium is the message."*[107] [My emphasis.]

This invested interest in violence was clearly illustrated during the Convention with the reports of TV crews asking demonstrators to "fake injuries" for the cameras. Wyoming Democratic Senator Gale McGee and his wife said that during the violence they personally saw at least one case where this took place. The police, however, had five specific complaints against the press:

1. Using TV lights which on one hand momentarily blinded officers, while on the other making them illuminated targets for riot rock throwers.

---

[106] *Rights in Conflict*, p. 304.
[107] Richard Strout, "News Media 'Prepare' Chicago for Violence," *Christian Science Monitor* (August 27, 1968).

2. Refusal to obey police officers.
3. Interfering with police duties.
4. Staging fake injuries of demonstrators.
5. Newsmen's mode of dress made it difficult for the police to distinguish between them and demonstrators.

On the other hand, the mass media's representatives were irritated and angered by the restrictions of TV network coverage of the Convention's proceedings and by the roughing up of some TV floor reporters by Convention security officers.

While these restrictions were dictated in part by security, the city officials understood that the radicals and revolutionaries descending on Chicago would play to the TV cameras. The network commentators who bitterly complained about Convention floor restrictions did so in the belief that Mayor Daley was seeking to abort the freedom of the press.

Given this, combined with an already built-in bias toward the demonstrators, the TV networks tended to tailor their coverage, both at the Convention and in the streets, in a manner that reflected a hostility toward the city of Chicago and Mayor Daley. As Chicago *Sun-Times* TV critic Paul Malloy observed:

> I did not hear any commentators reflect on what it must feel like for a policeman to be struck in the teeth or on the skull by a rock or a golf ball implanted with nails.
>
> I did not hear any commentator show anger at the tauntings and the obscenities hurled at the policemen.
>
> Vice President Hubert Humphrey says he saw a policeman get "stabbed in the face with a broken beer bottle. Cutting his eyes, his face, for no reason at all." But television apparently did not see this, or similar scenes of brutality. . . .
>
> I did not see television networks send their correspondents to the various hospitals to interview injured policemen. It seems to me there would have been some interesting stories there—and interesting pictures for the nation to see, and ponder on.[108]

On the floor of the Convention, the bias toward the dissidents was clearly illustrated by the TV coverage. As

---

[108] Paul Malloy, Chicago *Sun-Times*, reprinted in *Congressional Record*, H8259 (September 4, 1968).

Newsweek columnist Kenneth Crawford later observed:

Television, perhaps without meaning to, constantly abetted the disrupters [on the floor] by playing up their activities. In its search for interest and sensation, TV naturally concentrated on the angry minorities. Even during the extraordinary debate on Vietnam [one which the doves had long demanded—Editor] well worth the nation's attention, the cameras were not constantly on the podium. The result was a distortion that did the Democrats and their convention something less than full justice.[109]

Brains and Balance—Not Bias

The mass media's coverage of the Chicago disorders demonstrated both the bias of the media and the absence of any intelligent and thoughtful approach to a news story. Criticism of its bias in favor of dissident groups who demonstrated and often initiated violence continues to be regarded by the press as "carping," or the expression of overt or covert racism, or resentment toward the young and "progressive" forces in American society. This is evading the central factor so vividly illustrated in the coverage of Chicago: its built-in bias toward such groups. The press has yet to come to grips with a problem that can only be resolved with an intelligent approach, a conscious effort for balance, and a realization that the majority of Americans—middle-America—are the readers and viewers of their press reports and that middle-America appreciates honesty and is capable of its own individual evaluation of events if told the truth. Middle-America need not be talked down to or spoon-fed a singular point of view.

It is a fact that civil rights, peace demonstrators, student protests, and other dissenting groups are legitimate news. But it is equally true that the ends of responsible journalism are not served if only one side of an issue is presented.

For example, on the NBC "Today" show, in the wake of the Chicago violence, the show's host, Hugh Downs, did not serve the cause of intelligent balance by opining that "I guess, after all, the Chicago police are pigs." Even worse, later in the same show David Dellinger, Rennie Davis, and Tom Hayden were presented on the program, but there were not any officials of the city of Chicago. Film clips were run in the

---

[109] "Sore Losers," *Newsweek* (September 9, 1968).

news portion of the "Today" show, but no invitation was extended (to my knowledge) nor was the same amount of time provided for an opposing point of view to some of the downright falsehoods presented by the three major planners and movers of the mobs in Chicago.

Of equal, if not critical, importance, is the need of the media to have a thorough understanding of what the initiators of street action represent and just what are their goals. If the American mass media continues to walk the current path of bias, it could end up hopelessly compromising its role as the instrument of informing the American people.

Every reporter, editor, and TV reporter has his own opinions about matters of social policy. But Chicago demonstrated what happens when the media confuses its role as reporter with one as advocate of a particular point of view: the result is aiding and abetting social disorder. In the process, such an explosive situation does not help to clarify, but only beclouds, the picture the American people must have of current events if they are to remain a free people.

XI
The Misreading of Revolution: What Mayor Daley Did Wrong

"Had they sought to control the demonstrators," wrote New York *Times* columnist Tom Wicker of Mayor Daley, the police, and the city of Chicago,

> ... by cooperating with them in granting them elementary rights of marching and demonstrating, instead of repressing them by force, there need have been nothing like the brute spectacle millions of Americans witnessed on their television screens. ...
> They did not threaten law and order in Chicago, not if ordinary police prudence, common sense, and legal procedure had been exercised. The truth is that these were *our children in the streets, and the Chicago police beat them up.*[110] [My emphasis.]

It is a fact, which Wicker and others ignored, that no matter what concessions were made, the organizers of the disruption in Chicago were bent on violence. It is true that the Chicago rioters were "our children" (children of the middle class). But Wicker as well as Mayor Daley and the Chicago police totally misread the revolution going on in the streets, and for wholly different reasons.

Wicker and others sympathetic to the demonstrators regarded them as "legitimate." Mayor Daley regarded them as illegal, monolithic, and criminals. Both assessments are wrong. The longshoreman philosopher Eric Hoffer, a member of the Presidential Commission on the Causes and prevention of violence was more to the point when he warned:

> The Chicago riot was a preview of the future. Like Hitler they are going to take everything apart. *Those who think of Chicago's hippie rioters as children are now in for trouble.*[111] [My emphasis.]

---

[110]"The Question at Chicago," *The New York Times* (September 1, 1968).
[111]"Sees Warning in Chicago Riots," New York *Daily News* (September 1, 1968).

Mousetrapping Mayor Daley

"Mayor Daley was baited into a booby trap," wrote *Christian Science Monitor* Editor-in-Chief Erwin D. Canham.

> . . . The disrupters have scored a great triumph. They made their plans skillfully and the authorities fell into the ambush. The picture of Chicago and of the Democratic Convention sent everywhere is that of a party and candidate who required police state protection.[112]

In this contention Canham is correct. Mayor Daley did fall into a trap baited by Dellinger, Hayden, Rubin, and others. He is wrong, however, in insisting that the massive show of force—the marshalling of so much police and military manpower—was an exercise in overkill. As a matter of fact, the one decision that Daley made that was correct was the early show of force. It was this very show of force which New Left radicals like Jerry Rubin bitterly complained kept thousands of potential troublemakers away from the city during the Convention. No more than ten thousand radicals, Yippies, and McCarthy supporters engaged the police and National Guardsmen. Daley's twenty-one thousand police, National Guardsmen, and stand-by Federal troops were consistent with the rule of thumb established in matters of counterinsurgency and riot control: a ratio of two to one. To Mayor Daley's credit, this minimized the danger to the city, the Convention, life, and property.

But if the city did anything wrong, it was the deployment and use of the means at its disposal. For example, the police bore the brunt of the mob's provocation, often working in twelve to sixteen-hour shifts. This prolonged duty greatly contributed to the short tempers of the police. The Guard, on the other hand, was used in most, but not all, cases for relief of the police. It remains puzzling that the city of Chicago did not use the Guard and police interchangeably in, say, four-hour shifts. This would have minimized fatigue of the police forces and at the same time thrown the strategy of the demonstrators into confusion.

Ideally, the use of U.S. Marshalls—as with the Pentagon March in October 1967—in concert with the Chicago police

---

[112] "Overkill in Chicago," *Christian Science Monitor* (August 30, 1968).

and Guard would have helped in the riot control. U.S. Marshalls are professional riot police. None were present in the front lines in Chicago. It would have been much more sophisticated to confront the troublemakers in the streets and parks with "teams" of police, Guardsmen, and Marshalls, representing a united front of city, state, and federal authority.

Sleeping in the Park: A Crucial Ploy

Strategically it was an error for the city to try to enforce the Lincoln and Grant Park curfews; such insistence provided the pretext for violence the rioters wanted and needed. Many critics of Mayor Daley have argued this point but for fundamentally wrong reasons.

Effective riot control and crowd dispersal is for the express purpose of breaking up crowds and dispersing people to their homes. The thousands of demonstrators who went to Chicago had no homes in the nearby areas—which the radical MOB organizers had counted on. Driving the Yippies and other demonstrators from the park only sent them into the streets to smash windows and, later, they drifted back into the same park that had been cleared hours before.

There should be a cardinal rule of law enforcement in a crisis situation: do not attempt to enforce what is unenforceable. Abbie Hoffman, a Yippie leader, understood well the issue of "sleeping in the park" as the key to the plans for disruption. He wrote later in his book, *Revolution for the Hell of It:*

> We won the battle of Chicago. . . . I knew we had smashed the Democrats' chances. . . .
> All the way on the plane [returning to New York] I kept wondering what the f–k we would have done if they had let us stay in Lincoln Park at night. *As usual the cops took care of the difficult decisions.*[113]

It would have proven to be a shrewd and sophisticated move if the city of Chicago had not only opened the parks to the Yippies—thus splitting them off from, or at least breaking up, the radical troublemakers—but in conjunction with the National Guard had set up field soup kitchens, calling them "Daley's Diners." It is this kind of bizarre move which would have appealed to the less radical Yippies and hippies. It would have also helped to modify the image of Daley and the

[113]*Revolution for the Hell of It* (New York; Dial Press, 1968), pp. 114-115.

city of Chicago, built up in the radical underground press and the general media weeks before the Convention as a stern and humorless political boss and boss-ridden municipality.

If this smacks of advocating appeasement, remember that appeasement is usually a substitute for sound policy, and sound policy flows from an understanding of what you are faced with in a potential civil disorder. The city of Chicago's rigidity of policy and apparent belief that all demonstrators in Grant and Lincoln Parks were out to burn down the city produced a false and misleading impression to the nation and the world that the city and America were a "garrison state."

Mayor Daley and the city's representatives reflected in their policies and statements, as well as in their later-published report and television program, a fundamental lack of understanding of what they had been up against. They knew that many had come to Chicago to make trouble and to try to ignite a riot—but beyond this, their actions clearly showed the absence of an intelligent strategy to cope with the different groups who sought to sleep in Grant Park.

Also, Daley failed to make his own case for the measures taken or planned (that is, for example, calling in the National Guard) to the press, and thus to the public, very early. Rather, he waited until the end of the week and then became very defensive. Strategically, prior to the Convention week, Daley should have spelled out in a press conference the extent of the planning to try to disrupt the Convention—and at that time served notice to the news media that the city of Chicago did not want to hear any charges of police brutality if it was compelled to put down a potentially riotous situation. The press would then have been on notice that it would have been unwise to be in the middle of such a clash should it occur.

The Strategy of the Nightstick

Noted a police inspector from the city of Los Angeles who was on the scene as an observer:

> There is no question but that many officers acted without restraint and exerted force beyond that necessary under the circumstances. The leadership at the point of conflict did little to prevent such conduct and direct control of officers by first-line supervisors was virtually non-existent.[114]

---

[114] *Rights in Conflict, op. cit.,* p. 257.

The central flaw in all the complaints about the Chicago police is that they have either stemmed from political motivation or a complete ignorance of what the police faced in the streets of Chicago. Very little thoughtful analysis of what the police did wrong and why, and what will remedy a similar situation in the future, has been offered.

Almost everyone agrees that the police, in many instances, lost control during crucial periods of Convention week. One reason, however, is that the police were faced with a novel strategic situation and were unprepared to deal with it—for the Convention week disorders were not just like any past urban riots. To some extent, they were like the protests at Columbia in April 1968, which showed the emergence of the technique of verbal abuse of police over a sustained period of time. This technique was successfully applied in Chicago by some of the same people who had been at Columbia. Yet the performance of the Chicago police showed that they were not prepared, psychologically, for the abusive language and obscene references to their wives and daughters shouted at them by the demonstrators.

The lack of sophisticated training for Chicago police was also reflected in their use of clubs and riot batons. They could have learned some valuable lessons from the U.S. Marshalls at the Pentagon. Using the riot baton as an instrument for crowd dispersal, U.S. Marshalls aim for the lower parts of the body to disable a street thug and put him out of action; blows to the forearms, solar plexis, and legs leave a rioter immobilized and perhaps bruised, but unbloodied. As a result, a crumpled but unbloodied rioter does not offer an exciting picture for television and still cameramen.

The rioters wanted blood flowing from their heads for the benefit of the cameras. Although a review of the injured demonstrators shows that no one was injured seriously, the police "beating on heads" and the bloody pictures on TV and in newspapers gave the false impression that the police were conducting a massacre. Disciplined use of the riot batons would have minimized the bloody news photos of police action necessary to control the park and street riots that were in process. New York *Daily News* police reporter William Federici indicates that the police in Chicago, compared to those in New York, showed the absence of discipline and understanding of crowd control. He contends that in Chicago it was "club control." He wrote:

The Chicago cops were taunted, but so are New York cops. I've heard the taunts, a lot of them, worse than I heard here [in Chicago]. But in New York the cops await an order before taking action. In Chicago they swing their club, then tell the sargeant. . . .

Chicago cops apparently are not trained to use only "necessary force." To them an order to "move them back" is an order to smash through the first ten rows of people in front of them, beating everyone along the way.

The New York way to push a mob back is shoulder-to-shoulder, pushing hard, not clubbing. The New York cop's nightstick—when he has it—is usually behind his partner's back.[115]

Handcuffed City and Cops

In the final analysis, however, the city of Chicago and its police force lacked one of the principal weapons which politicians throughout the nation have been loath to provide: city, state, or federal laws which clearly define the still-murky area between civil disobedience (the prelude to violence) and incitement to riot. Throughout the civil turmoil and riots of the 1960s, political and civic leaders have been unable to draw a clear line between legitimate dissent and civil disobedience. This failure stems from the political peril the leadership believes such a definition implies and from a woeful amount of ignorance about the differences between the two. Radicals, revolutionaries, and protestors bent on inciting violence have used the thin line between civil disobedience and dissent, and the confusion that pervades the issue, for their own power purposes.

Stated generally, city, state, and federal officals will soon have to put on the statute books a law that makes it a crime to advocate by word or deed the initiation of physical force, or threats of such force, by either an individual or groups of individuals, to achieve a specific political, moral, or social objective. Such a proposed law should spell out that dissent ends and civil disobedience begins when such threats of force or actual force come into play. And such a definition does not contravene the First Amendment of freedom of speech or assembly.

Time and again the courts have ruled on cases which involve the famous phrase that freedom of speech does not

---

[115]"Chicago Cops, N.Y. Cops—Miles Apart," New York *Daily News* (August 30, 1968).

mean the freedom to cry "fire" in a crowded theater. In effect, revolutionaries and New Left radicals who hide behind free speech and assembly do so because city councils, state legislatures, and the U.S. Congress have not had the moral courage to face up to defining this important principle and to drawing the demarcation between legitimate freedom to exercise disapproval of policy of those in power, and the license to incite or commit actual acts of anarchy and riot.

No city, state, or nation can long remain ordered and free, with its citizens and property inviolable, if organized minorities are allowed to use the pretext of freedom of speech and assembly to incite mobs to violence and anarchy.

If the city of Chicago, the state government of Illinois, or the federal Government had had laws clearly forbidding the expression of, or the initiation of, force to achieve a political, social, or moral objective, ample evidence was available, prior to Chicago's Democratic Convention, to arrest and hold for prosecution and trial David Dellinger, Abbie Hoffman, Jerry Rubin, Tom Hayden, and other political gangsters who went to Chicago.

Lacking such a legal weapon, framed within reason and individual liberty, the city of Chicago and the police were needlessly handcuffed, as have been all law enforcement officials since civil turmoil began mounting in the early 1960s.

Thus the radicals who went to Chicago came off with a howling success, largely achieved by the default of the established leadership to understand just what it faced.

Art Goldberg, coordinator of the National Mobilization Committee (the MOB) later wrote that the MOB's goals were "successful beyond the wildest dreams of the organizers":

> To judge the enormity of the achievement, one must realize there were no more than 5,000 active demonstrators in the city at any one time. [We would say 10,000 if you count the McCarthy supporters and the idle and curious young.] Yet these 5,000 people, *aided by the McCarthy delegates inside the Convention*, were able to turn Chicago into a garrison state, and to effectively disrupt the Democratic Party's Festival of Death.
>
> More than that, the demonstrators have managed to disrupt the Establishment. The mass media is warring with Mayor Daley and the Democratic machine. Liberal and conservative Democrats are at each other's throats.

"One of the jobs of the revolutionary," says Jerry Rubin, *"is to split the Establishment. We accomplished that in Chicago."*[116] [My emphasis.]

[116]"Chicago One: The Convention from the Outside," New York *Free Press* (September 5, 1968).

XII
The Walker Report: A Document of Self-Deception

The right to dissent is fundamental to democracy. But the expression of that right has become one of the most serious problems in contemporary democratic government. That dilemma was dramatized in Chicago during the Democratic National Convention of 1968—*the dilemma of a city coping with the expression of dissent.*[117] [My emphasis.]

Thus begins a report that purports to offer the story of what took place during the most traumatic week in the recent history of American political life. Yet the evidence the Walker Report presents sharply conflicts with its summation and conclusions.

At the very onset the Walker Report makes the major mistake of confusing dissent with what actually took place in Chicago: deliberate acts of provocation that precipitated a "political riot." As the columnist James Jackson Kilpatrick pointed out in a thoughtful article on the Walker Report:

The error lies in the implication that the Chicago demonstrators were engaged in nothing more than an "expression of dissent. . . ."
It is ludicrous to suggest that this criminal conduct was in any way whatever an "expression of dissent." It was not free speech, not free press, not peaceable assembly. The dilemma as defined by the Commission's staff was not the dilemma that confronted Chicago. The problem was rather in coping with massive public disorders deliberately fomented by young revolutionaries who had no intention of respecting law or public safety.[118]

In the Tradition of Past Reports
The Walker Report follows in the footsteps of the Kerner and Warren Commissions' studies: each is impressive in the supposed scope of investigation, but each fails to integrate its mass of facts into a comprehensive view that provides a

[117] *Rights in Conflict, op. cit.,* Forward, p. xv.
[118] "That Walker Report," *Human Events* (December 14, 1968).

glimpse of the *real* causes behind the murder of an American President, urban riots, and the disorders of Chicago. Lacking these answers, the Commissions of the last few years have been loath even to suggest that behind such events may very well be a dedicated revolutionary minority using assassination, social disorders, and violence to weaken the social fabric of the United States.

In the case of the Warren and Kerner Commissions' reports, both were released in Presidential election years and seemed calculated to serve political ends instead of informing a bewildered and confused citizenry as to why America since 1963 has experienced the most serious and continual volume of domestic violence in this century.

Each report advances arguments that are impossible to prove or based on untenable theories. The Warren Commission used the single-bullet theory to substantiate its thesis that Lee Harvey Oswald acted alone. In the case of the Kerner Commission, it cited "white racism" as the cause of the riots. And the Walker Report confused dissent with calculated civil disobedience and willful intent to foment unrest toward the goal of political revolution.

Thus, what we are left with is a vast credibility gap between the nation's government leadership and its citizenry. As the national business and financial weekly, *Barron's*, observed in an editorial on the Walker Report findings:

> What exists . . . is perhaps the worst credibility gap in U.S. history, one to which a number of Presidential Commissions have contributed. . . .
> . . . The Walker Report stands hopelessly inpugned. Because of widespread leaks, publishers were able to come out with a paperback version a week after its official release; the same circumstances helped pressure approval (for its publication, not its contents) from the members of the Commission, most of whom received only a hurried glance at a copy and who feared otherwise they would be charged with suppressing information. . . .
> *With the best will in the world—and that's a doubtful proposition—Presidential Commissions seem incapable of "telling it like it is." Tax-supported bias is no substitute for the truth.*[119] [My emphasis.]

---

[119] "Bias Run Riot," *Barron's* (December 16, 1968).

The Politics of the Walker Report

The truth of the Walker Report, whether Chicago attorney Daniel Walker wished it or not, is that the timing and manner of its release left it not only impugned but discredited as an official objective Government study.

Chicago Chief Judge William J. Campbell, who impaneled a Federal grand jury to look into the disorders that had engulfed the Democratic Convention, contended that "I question both the timing and motivation behind the timing," asserting that its release appeared calculated to influence the grand jury, if not to undercut its effectiveness.[120]

Campbell also revealed that on October 3, 1968, Walker promised him that he would submit a rough draft of the report on the Chicago disorders to permit removal of information that might compromise the work of the impaneled grand jury. That promise, according to Campbell, was broken by Walker, and Campbell claims he did not know the substance of the report until summaries appeared in newspapers like the New York *Times*, which headlined:

U.S. STUDY SCORES CHICAGO
VIOLENCE AS "POLICE RIOT"

In a conversation with Walker just prior to the release of the Report, Campbell states:

> "When I reminded him of the agreement, he said there was no such agreement. When I told him release of the report could cause difficulty with the grand jury, he assured me that the Attorney General [at the time, Ramsey Clark] had already taken steps to protect grand jury interests.
>
> "I asked Mr. Walker how the Attorney General knew what the interests of the grand jury were since I didn't know and no indictments had been returned."
>
> Judge Campbell quoted Mr. Walker as saying that *aides of the Attorney General had provided some information on the grand jury investigation to Mr. Clark's office.*
>
> *"That was definitely wrong,"* Judge Campbell said. *"This violates the secrecy of the grand jury, and it is not the proper way to proceed."*[121] [My emphasis.]

It was not widely reported that Attorney General Ramsey Clark actively lobbied for Daniel Walker to head the probe,

---

[120] The New York *Times* (December 5, 1968).
[121] "Chicago Judge Accuses Walker of Breaking Personal Promise," The New York *Times* (December 9, 1968).

which was conducted at the request of the Presidential Commission on the Causes and Preventions of Violence. The importance of this fact is that the Chicago *Tribune* leveled the charge that the summary of the report was rewritten by Ramsey Clark to conform with the official Justice Department line: that the police were responsible for the disorders in Chicago and not the radicals and revolutionaries. Clark had pursued this delusive line during his short tenure as Johnson's Attorney General, alleging that urban and campus disorders were not premeditated, and he had refused to return indictments against black and white radicals who were clearly implicated in the continual waves of violence.

That the summary, which included the indictment of the Chicago police as creating a "police riot," was rewritten appears strongly possible in that there is a clear conflict between the body of the Report and the summary.

The body presents overwhelming information about what the police were faced with and the extensive preparation employed by the radicals. But in the Report's summary, the predominance of blame falls on the shoulders of the police.

Undercutting the National Commission

There are further indications that politics played a large part in at least the summary of the Walker Report. Daniel Walker is the former aide to the late Adlai Stevenson, whose son has headed up an Illinois political faction that has sought to depose Mayor Richard Daley. The Presidential Commission on the Causes and Prevention of Violence for which the Report was intended, furthermore, had its role preempted by the release of the Report to the press and to various publishing houses before the Commission members had had more than a hasty glance at its conclusions. They had little choice but to give their sanction when the summary was leaked to the press. The *fait accompli* of Walker and his staff was such that it would put the Commission members, if they objected, in the position of being charged with trying to suppress information. As two Commission members put it, "Had we suppressed the report we would have been damned forever," and it would have "found its way into print anyway."[122]

However, Arizona State Supreme Court Justice Ernest W. McFarland, a member of the Commission, said that he argued

----

[122] The New York *Times* (December 5, 1968).

in vain with the Commission's chairman, Dr. Milton Eisenhower, that the Report not be made public until the members of the Commission had had time to study the Report fully and that he feared it would "stir up hard feelings and hatred."[123] Justice McFarland commented:

> I was fearful that mere release of information of this nature would tend to give it substantiation. One of the reasons I felt that we should not release the report was that *many of the statements made were not sworn statements, and in many instances the names of the parties were not given.*[124] [My emphasis.]

Combined with the possibility of violation of the secrecy of the Grand Jury, the absence of professional legal procedure cast the Walker Report in further disrepute. Added to these factors was Walker's defense of the manner and method of release. For example, in defending his action Walker pleaded that he was releasing the report because of a mid-November 1968 deadline given by the Commission—yet he all but ignored this body and appears to have gone over its head in his cooperation with certain organs of the mass media and the press. Ironically, Dr. Eisenhower was forced to issue a statement that the very Commission which had ordered the study found that the Report did reflect the view of that Commission!

Press Agentry of the Report

The skill employed by the Walker group to circumvent the Presidential Commission was vividly illustrated by how the report was leaked. First, it was timed to catch prime-time Sunday news coverage. Second, the paperback publisher, in addition to the New York *Times* and *Life* magazine, had advance copies of the Report! *Life* in its December 6, 1968, issue carried a summary and with it a companion piece alleging payoffs to the Chicago police. The caption of the article read, "YOU CAN'T EXPECT POLICE ON THE TAKE TO TAKE ORDERS"—a reference to the breakdown of individual police discipline during the height of the disorders at the Convention.

Later, at a press conference, Walker did not dispell the suspicion that behind the Report's release was an attempt to in-

---

[123] *Ibid.*
[124] *Ibid.*

dict Mayor Daley, the Chicago police, and the political organization Daley heads as responsible for the disorders. Walker
asserted that what contributed to the disorders was Mayor
Daley's earlier, April 1968 order to "shoot to kill arsonists"
and "shoot to maim looters." From Walker's view, these statements conditioned the Chicago police to act with violence.[125]

The Chicago attorney demanded that police guilty of brutality be punished but, like McCarthy and other politicians, he
made no statement asserting that the rioters and revolutionaries be punished for provoking the police into action or for
any acts of violence and property destruction on their part.

What Is Really Wrong with the Walker Report

The failure of the Walker Report is really a failure of men
such as Walker and Ramsey Clark to face the fact that Chicago and other disorders since the Kennedy assassination of
November 1963 were the work of a revolutionary movement
intent on bringing America to its knees.

Besides confusing dissent with disorder, the Report reflects
a woeful ignorance of the nature of these revolutionaries; like
professors and college administrators, Walker and others still
think in terms of earlier civil rights protests when they should
be reading Marcuse, Guevara, Frantz Fannon, and other Leftist or Communist luminaries from whom the New Left draws
its major philosophical inspiration.

Most important, in the Report's summary that Chicago
was a "police riot," no attempt is made to offer suggestions
of how the police, in the future, can cope with the type of
premeditated disorders which overwhelmed the political process in August 1968. All Walker could do was demand that
the policemen responsible be punished and state that even
this would not be enough.

What is wrong with the Walker Report is what is wrong
with most of the political, intellectual, and moral leadership
in America today: it cannot face the tragic fact that its past
permissive policies helped create the violent era of the 1960s,
and it lacks the courage to cope effectively with the problem
—which means it suffers from a conditioned way of thinking
that stares reality in the face and chooses to call it something
other than what it is.

Contained in the summary by Daniel Walker is the assump-

---

[125] *Time* (December 13, 1968).

tion that the radicals and student-adult revolutionaries had "freedom and peace" in mind when they went to Chicago. But overwhelming evidence in the body of the report leads one to conclude just the opposite. It is this kind of delusive thinking that has produced a form of self-disarmament in America's intellectual, political, and moral leadership. And as a result of this delusive disarmament, individual freedom and security from violence are now in grave peril.

XIII
Taking the Party to the Undemocratic Left

"A lot of things will never be the same after this week," commented MOB organizer David Dellinger after Chicago.
After this week, the kids have got a sense of their own strength. [The activists will return home] to create 200, 300 Chicagos. This does not mean that it will follow the same pattern, but we will expose the repressive machinery of military power.
We can have more impact in the streets and in resistance movements than by playing electoral politics.[126] [My emphasis.]

Tom Hayden and Rennie Davis made similar boasts. Hayden stated, "There's coming a time when the American movement will become more violent for defensive and survival reasons."[127] Davis vowed that after Chicago "we expect a lot of action at universities, there will be Columbias all over the country."[128]

And at Berkeley, San Francisco State, the University of Wisconsin, New York University, Brandeis, and other major universities violence erupted between October 1968 and the spring of 1969. But attempts to disrupt the election and the inauguration of Richard Nixon as follow-ups to Chicago fizzled.

Left unanswered, however, is the fate and future of the Democratic Party in the wake of the violence of Convention week—particularly the role the New Left radicals will play inside as well as outside the party.

"Toward a Democratic Left"
Two Socialist writers in the magazine *Dissent* wrote:

Perhaps the most hopeful accomplishment of the Left in the last three and a half years is the shift it has forced in the rhetoric of political discourse. . . .

---

[126]"Radicals, Relaxing on Illinois Farm, Relive Chicago," *The New York Times* (September 1, 1968).
[127]*Ibid.*
[128]*Ibid.*

Suddenly the "new politics" is reflected "within" the established parties! Political candidates speaking of expanding "participation"; they debate "black power" and the "guaranteed annual income. . . ."[129]

These Socialists and the more radical leftists understand the impact and influence the New Left has had, and can have in the future, in pushing the major political parties farther to the Left, beyond the welfare state by degrees to state Socialism. They also understand how violence can be utilized to speed their goal. The Democratic Party, traditionally, has been the most radical of the two national parties. Since the days of Franklin Roosevelt it has been the conveyor belt for the building blocks of the welfare state in America.

Now in a crisis, the turning point in Chicago, the party faces the prospect of having nowhere to go but farther to the Left. Indeed, even before the Convention one of the major architects of Lyndon Johnson's "war on poverty," Socialist Michael Harrington, told the nation that America has no choice but to go beyond the welfare state. Before the Democratic Convention, Harrington wrote in *Toward a Democratic Left*:

> Last generation's reforms will not solve this generation's crisis, for all the official figures prove that it is *now necessary to go beyond Franklin Roosevelt*. . . . The country has no choice but to have some larger ideas and take them seriously. . . . Liberalism, as it has been known for these three decades, cannot respond to challenge *unless it moves sharply to the democratic left*.[130] [My emphasis.]

Shift, Not Seizure, of the Party

If regular Democrats and "law and order" Liberals fear a seizure of the party by delegates of the National Conference for New Politics, who were behind the Convention disruption and outside in the streets, it is fear founded on fantasy and flies in the face of past political history. Much more dangerous to the Democratic Party's "Old Politics"—meaning the coalition put together since the days of the New Deal—is the likelihood of a shift to the more extreme political Left to win

---

[129] William Connolly and Arnold S. Kaufman, "Between Exaltation & Despair," *Dissent* (September-October, 1968).
[130] Michael Harrington, *Toward a Democratic Left* (New York; Macmillan, 1968).

elections and the support of the intellectuals and the mass media. Helping along in this regard will be those "New Politics" leaders who have not given up their aim to either smash the party or control it. As a national magazine observed a few weeks after the election:

> Some political insiders claim that the turmoil going on in the Democratic Party today is aimed more at the control of the party for the *1972 convention rather than the election of a President in 1968.*
>
> In their view, Kennedy and McCarthy partisans are trying to take over the party machinery at the State, congressional-district and local levels for the purpose of writing their own ticket and platform in another four years.[131] [My emphasis.]

In fact, four months after the disorders in Chicago it was revealed that many of the disruptive delegates were seeking to control the makeup of two standing commissions created by the Democratic Party at the 1968 Convention. "New Politics" advocates advanced the names of Adlai Stevenson III and Julian Bond, along with other Kennedy and McCarthy supporters, for one of the commissions.[132] Control of such committees would give the 1968 disruptive factions dictatorial control over the makeup and rules of the Convention—a power these same delegates at the 1968 Convention persistently decried as "boss rule" when they were not in control.

It was clear that the McCarthy and Kennedy coalition at the 1968 Convention represented a minority, as indicated by the fate of their Convention "peace platform." But this presents no barrier to their supporters who are playing the game of rule-or-ruin politics within the party.

This was clearly demonstrated during the Humphrey presidential campaign after the Convention. Although the then Vice President was beset by New Left demonstrators at major campaign stops, members of the "New Politics" were either sitting on their hands or meeting—plotting how to come off with control of the party after Humphrey's defeat in November. One such meeting in October 1968 was attended by

---

[131] "Fourth Party: Is the Real Target '68—or Democratic Control in '72?" *U.S. News & World Report* (September 16, 1968).

[132] "Democratic Fight Looms Over Commission That Could Influence Make-up of '72 National Convention," The New York *Times* (December 1, 1968).

McCarthy and Kennedy supporters, among them McCarthy's campaign architect, Allard Lowenstein. Their strategy was "based on the belief that it will be easier to recapture control of the party if the Vice President is beaten this fall."[133]

And, indeed, the image of the party at the Convention in August—one of chaos, confusion, and "police state repression," which some of these very "New Politics" delegates had created—was too much for Humphrey to overcome and undoubtedly aided in his defeat. Shortly afterward, the New Democratic Coalition began springing up in cities across the country, specifically in suburban Washington, D.C., St. Louis, Illinois, New York, and California—places where dissident delegates had their major strength.

Paul Wieck, in *The New Republic*, estimates that this coalition is organized in twenty-five of the fifty states, with relatively strong organizations in eighteen—many of these in metropolitan centers of the nation.[134]

Thus, while many younger Democrats still think of themselves as Liberals, in reality they are something more than the kind of Liberal that has dominated traditional party politics since FDR. In calling themselves members of the "New Politics" they have taken Liberalism farther to the left.

Nixon, Kennedy, and the "New Politics"

In the breakup of the "Old Politics" of the Democratic Party, and the little-discussed political shift caused by the Chicago riots, President Richard M. Nixon and Senator Edward M. Kennedy are not to remain untouched between now and 1972. A national news magazine wrote a month after Nixon was sworn in as President:

> Politicians now predict the development of an unspoken rivalry during the next four years, in which political commentators inevitably will compare what Republican Richard Nixon is doing at the White House with what Democratic Edward Kennedy is saying in the U.S. Senate.
>
> Just as Lyndon Johnson kept a close watch on the political maneuvers of Robert Kennedy and his backers, so Mr. Nixon is likely to be keenly aware of what Ted

---

[133] New York *Post* (September 16, 1968).
[134] "The New Politics Still Lives," *The New Republic* (September, 1968).

Kennedy is doing and tailor the Administration's program accordingly.[135]

During his first few months in office Nixon showed a willingness to minimize the differences between himself and Ted Kennedy. Like his brother Robert, who stayed politically left of Lyndon Johnson, Ted Kennedy must stay left of Nixon to hold the Democratic Party regulars and at the same time appeal to the members of the "New Politics." A close aide of John and Robert and now Ted Kennedy asserted even before Hubert Humphrey's defeat that "Old Politics" must give way to the "New." Historian Arthur Schlesinger, Jr., went on to state that "the Democrats will have no choice but to face the bitter question of how to revive and rebuild their party."[136] It cannot go to the right, which Nixon supposedly has laid claim to, thus it must move farther to the left, or in Schlesinger's words, "In short, the Old Politics of the middlemen is now giving way to the New Politics of mass involvement."[137] Eugene McCarthy in 1968 showed the way, as Schlesinger correctly acknowledges.

However, Richard Nixon is intent on making the GOP a majority party. To do this he must try to win the favor of the all-important Liberal news media and influential segments of the intellectual and academic community who look with considerable approval on the "New Politics." But Nixon is in a box since the members of the "New Politics" demonstrated their willingness to employ violence; also during the term of LBJ, witness their violent opposition to the Vietnam war when their political wishes were not followed.

The conservative Republicans, on the other hand, believe that Nixon is abandoning the pledges he made during the 1968 campaign. If, therefore, Nixon tries to be all things to all people, he may find himself in the same position Lyndon Johnson was in two years after his 1964 landslide victory: the victim of attacks from all sides. Like Johnson, Nixon may find little support for unpopular policies.

---

[135] "As Kennedy Plans for 1972," *U.S. News & World Report* (February 24, 1969).
[136] "The Future Democratic Party," *New York Magazine* (November 4, 1968).
[137] *Ibid.*

The Tyranny of the Minority

Out of these political circumstances emerges an explosive and perhaps unprecedented situation in American political history. Without question the 1968 election showed a considerable shift to the political right in America; the Gallup, Harris, and other polls showed this as much as did the combined votes for George C. Wallace and Nixon. More precisely, the 1968 election was a repudiation of the Liberal welfare state doctrine—less due to ideology, and more due to the weariness of the mass of Americans in paying for its mounting costs. But this is hardly reflected in the actions of Nixon and Kennedy, who are both vying for the minority support of the Liberal intellectuals and members of the press.

What we now have, which has been developing for a number of years, are politicians promising one thing to the voters during elections and delivering just the opposite between elections in order to appease vocal Liberal intellectuals, socio-economic-political commentators, and members of the press (all of whom believe that they know what is best for the masses). In a phrase, we have come to have electoral politics of the minority tyrannizing the majority. If such a state of severe alienation between the mass of Americans—middle-America—and the political leadership continues, we are likely to witness a violent explosion of majority rage against such minority dictation. Already there is talk in the press of a "taxpayers' revolt." If such frustrations find no relief or outlet, no one can say whether or not a mass of middle-America citizens will not in the end emulate the New Left and go into the streets, or follow a leader who promises to make all things right with the force of a nightstick.

It is just such an explosion that the New Left not only wants, but is working to create. It is putting pressure on the Democratic Party to go farther to the left, knowing that, as in the past, Republicans will follow suit. The Republicans have never understood how to fight consistently the drift of the American political process toward greater welfare statism or the interventionism of the State in the lives of Americans. Also, the Republican Party undoubtedly believes that it is the advocacy of such policies that has made the Democratic Party the majority party for over thirty years; it fails to place the blame on its own inability to articulate alternate policies.

The Second American Revolution

It is clear that regular Democrats and Republicans have no idea of the real aim of the New Left. They did not understand the dangerous import of Chicago in August 1968, or the purpose behind the urban and campus unrest between 1964 and 1968. Both are part of an attempt, such as that in Germany in the 1920s and 1930s, to carry the country *beyond* the welfare state. As the New Left publication *Guardian* phrased it after Nixon's election:

> Today's crisis in America is a fantastic opportunity for our movement, but only if we fully and without illusion understand both the crisis and our relationship to it as a revolutionary force. . . .
> We must begin to understand not only capitalism as an economic system, but how it insinuates itself into every aspect of American life. . . .
> We do not believe anyone has fully analyzed the nature of capitalistic society or has developed a completely rational strategy for taking power from the ruling class. . . .
> The American revolution—as all revolutions—will be a variation on a theme of liberation and violent upheaval. . . .[138]

If there are those that contend "it can't happen here," the events at Chicago and the continuing violence on the nation's college campuses and in the cities in 1969 is tragic proof not only that it *can* happen, but violent and vivid proof that *it is happening here*.

Lacking any firm, intelligent, and consistent opposition, today's irrational nostrums of the New Left can be tomorrow's political policy and dogma. This is the way Nazism came to Germany, first taking the route of the welfare state, then going beyond it to National Socialism.

The welfare state has come to America by the same route: by degrees, determined propaganda, and intellectual and moral default.

---

[138] "The Forces Exist to Make a Beginning," *Guardian* (November 23, 1968).

XIV

The Welfare State: The Bridgehead to the Police State

We are deeply indebted to Herbert Spencer [nineteenth century critic and political seer] for recognizing with a sharper eye than any of his contemporaries, and warning them against, "the coming slavery" toward which the State of their own time was drifting, and toward which we are moving more swiftly today.

It is more than a grim coincidence that Spencer was warning of the coming slavery in 1884, and that George Orwell, in our time, has predicted that the full consummation of this slavery will be reached in 1984, exactly one century later.[139] [Economist Henry Hazlitt in *Man vs. the Welfare State*]

Most of the college generation of the 1960s has read George Orwell's *1984* and found it a powerful warning as to what happens when the all-powerful state takes over. But if they had been required to read Herbert Spencer's 1884 work, *The Man Versus the State*, they would marvel at the similarity of thought and dynamic quality of Spencer and Orwell, two of the most devastating British critics of Socialism. The similarity between Orwell and Spencer does not end with just intellectual insight; both men drew their conclusions from a vast fund of practical experience.

The lives of Orwell and Spencer were not spent in the ivory tower of intellectual thought and theory. Spencer was a railroad engineer and a magazine editor, and his associations were with men of equally practical and rugged life experience. Orwell moved among the masses of the poor to an even greater degree, while "down and out in London and Paris" (which he later wrote about in a book of that title), and while working as a colonial policeman in Burma.

What is particularly remarkable is that Spencer foresaw the rise of Communism, Nazism, and Fascism. More important, he saw the process through which such dictatorship would be

---

[139]*Man vs. the Welfare State, From Spencer's 1884 to Orwell's 1984*, to be published by Arlington House, excerpts reprinted in *Congressional Record*, E1891 (March 11, 1969).

created: the growth of the state over the individual in the
name of progress. He observed in *The Man Versus the State*:

> ... every additional State-interference strengthens
> the tacit assumption that it is the duty of the State to
> deal with all evils and secure all benefits. . . . The people
> at large, led to look on benefits received through public
> agencies as gratis benefits, have their hopes continually
> excited by the prospects of more. A spreading educa-
> tion, furthering the diffusion of pleasant errors rather
> than stern truths, renders such hopes both stronger and
> more general. Worse still, such hopes are ministered to
> by candidates for public choice. . . . Journalism, ever
> responsive to popular opinion, daily strengthens it by
> giving it voice; while counter-opinion, more and more
> discouraged, finds little utterance.
>
> ... It is said that the French Revolution devoured its
> own children. Here, analogous catastrophe seems not
> unlikely.[140]

—Not unlike the conditions in America today. And as
events proved in the following century, Spencer was quite
correct in seeing where such policies were heading. For the
Communist revolution of 1917 did, in the Stalinist purges,
"devour its children," and Hitler purged those who had
helped him to power in the 1920s and 1930s. The millions
murdered and maimed in the name of the Soviet or Nazi state
serve further to prove Spencer's point.

The Prelude to the Police State

Spencer put forth in *Man Versus the State* that it was reasonable to suppose welfare state policies of Britain and Europe in the latter nineteenth century were "the coming of
slavery" simply because "all Socialism involves slavery."
George Orwell was to observe that Socialism without freedom of choice meant Big Brother.

What is frightening is that the road to Big Brother involves
the issue of social conflict. The street and civil conflicts of
the 1960s in America are very similar to what happened prior
to World War I in Europe. For fourteen years prior to 1914
Europe was rocked with riots; also students and workers bat-
tled the police and army. Not unlike the New Left in Chicago
in August 1968, many of the leaders of such violent "con-

---

[140] Herbert Spencer, *The Man Versus the State* (London, 1892),
p. 314.

frontations" prior to 1914 were Marxist revolutionaries allied with the cause of Syndicalism. Syndicalism is a form of Communism that employs violence and the general strike as weapons to seize the existing economic and governmental institutions.

Syndicalism as a major political form is allegedly an action kind of group "participatory Democracy"—where supposedly the entire group of workers or students make political decisions. Today in America, Syndicalism is very much a promoted feature of the Students for a Democratic Society and is embraced by many radicals who were inside and outside the Democratic Convention in Chicago. While such a political form is said to exist within the SDS, in practice the SDS has more of an elitist rule with a few making decisions that the many follow.

The Marxists and Syndicalists prior to World War I were not seeking to take power from their philosophical enemies, the Capitalists. Their main fire was turned against Democratic Socialists—the forerunner of today's modern Liberal. The radicals had denounced the Democratic Socialists for "selling out Socialism" and settling instead for welfare and social programs. Like today's Liberals, the Democratic Socialists believed in the "mixed economy," part private enterprise and part government controls.

Just as today's believers in the American Welfare State refuse to see the consequences of their policies as the catalyst for social conflicts, so those Liberals prior to World War I refused to see how their welfare state created serious distortions in the mechanisms of the economic market. Out of its economic dislocation—fed by inflation because of wild government spending schemes—grew worker discontent and widespread strikes, urged on and organized in many cases, by Marxist revolutionaries.

In the end, the social conflict in Europe for years prior to World War I conditioned an entire continent to believe that violence and disruption were the way to settle political disputes. It was no coincidence that the assassination of the Austrian Archduke by Serbian student radicals in June 1914 provided the pretext for World War I.

The Decay and Drift Unabated

The drift toward statism via the welfare state did not end with World War I. In Germany, especially, the Weimar Republic adopted the "mixed economy" and the welfare state. At the same time there arose in Germany a generation of younger people embittered by the war they believed their elders had made possible. Much like America's hippies or Yippies of today, this generation of younger Germans (called *Jugenbewegung*) dressed in colorful, nonconformist clothing, strummed guitars, and wandered the German countryside singing folk songs and moaning that the older generation would not let them "be free."

Philosophically and politically they embraced the concepts of the welfare state and many gave their support to more radical measures of Socialism. Historians note that it was this political philosophy which provided Hitler's National Socialism "much of its dynamics of its earlier drive to power."[141]

A more startling parallel is the influence many German professors had on the educated youth prior to Hitler and the influence of the more liberal or radical professors in American universities today who have helped create the New Left. Historian William L. Shirer in *The Rise and Fall of the Third Reich* observes that the German professors prior to Hitler's regime had so infected the youth with a contempt for democracy, and had so encouraged the doctrine of anti-Semitism and National Socialism, that "by 1932 the majority of students appeared enthusiastic for Hitler."[142]

Thus, by 1933 the currents of thought in German life had paved the way for Hitler's Third Reich, which took Germany beyond the welfare state to full National Socialism.

Nazis Not the Only Dictators

Because of the magnitude of the barbarism of Nazism, historians have tended to ignore the fact that after World War I a rash of dictatorships erupted in every nation that sought to make the "mixed economy," or the welfare state, work. In the order of their appearance, dictatorships sprang up in Russia and Poland (1917), Italy (1922), Spain (1923), Turkey (1923), Chile (1927), Greece (1928), Japan (1929), Brazil (1930), the Dominican Republic (1930), Argentina (1931), Guatemala (1932), Uruguay (1933), Austria (1933), Germany (1933), and Mexico (1934).

---

[141] *The Hippies* (Time Inc., 1967), p. 162.
[142] William L. Shirer, *The Rise and Fall of the Third Reich* (Fawcett Crest; April, 1968), p. 347.

It is significant to point out that with the 1932 election of Franklin D. Roosevelt, the New Deal established policies which had been implemented in each of those countries prior to every one of the above dictatorships. More ironic is that America went to war against Germany, Italy, and Japan holding philosophical principles—however mild in form—almost identical to those regimes.

Making note of this, the late John T. Flynn, author of *The Roosevelt Myth*, argues that instead of calling its policies "fascism," the New Deal preferred to use the term "Planned Capitalism." Flynn observed:

> There was only one trouble with it. This is what Mussolini had adopted, the Planned Capitalist State, and he gave it a name—Facism. Then came Hitler and adopted the same idea. . . .
> Yet this curiously un-American doctrine was being peddled in America as the bright flower of the liberals. Of course they did not dare call it fascism, because that had a bad name. . . . They called it the Planned Economy. But it was and is fascism by whatever name it is known.[143]

Flynn also observes that World War I was the outgrowth of fifty years of European Socialism—which had begun to take hold a decade or so after the publication of Karl Marx's *Communist Manifesto*. And from the era of the Bismarck welfare state in Germany (circa 1870) to World War II—a period of seventy years—the growth of the Welfare State in Europe had been constant. He then cites four causes that made both World Wars I and II possible:

> (1) Extending social services beyond the capacity of the State to support; (2) using militarism as a means of employing men in the army and in the factories to supply the army; (3) paying for all this with vast government debts; and (4) the gradual extension of radical socialist ideas throughout Europe. The First World War interrupted but did not end these drifts. The new European government moved as fast as possible into militaristic programs. The left-wing parties were powerful in the governments and used that power to develop on a greater scale than ever the Welfare State, committed to jobs

---

[143] John T. Flynn, *The Roosevelt Myth*, revised ed. (New York; 1956), pp. 152-153.

and security for all. . . . What Hitler did in Germany,
Mussolini in Italy, Metaxas in Greece, and various other
dictators in other countries was merely the end result of
every attempt to set up the Welfare State. It cannot
work under a democratic government because it must
have a dictator to enforce its harsh policies. *The welfare
state cannot operate without the police state.*[144]

Conflict Between Freedom and Force

Each of the American political Administrations, beginning
with FDR and continuing through LBJ's Great Society, has
believed that it could force or plan the economic and social
destiny of the American people. Herbert Spencer understood
as early as 1884 that this could only lead to "slavery," as it
did less than twenty years after his own death in 1903. The
regimes of Roosevelt, Truman, Eisenhower, Kennedy, and
Johnson, and now Nixon, have rejected complete freedom in
favor of varying degrees of force. Now in the second half of
this century we see the rise of radical political forces that
would commit the same offenses as those of an earlier part of
this century.

Ominous in its implication is the parallel in timing, observed by Dr. Leonard Peikoff of Brooklyn College in a lecture series. The period of the welfare state under Bismarck
and the coming to power of Hitler and National Socialism
was roughly forty-five years. The period from the emergence
of the FDR New Deal in 1933 to the violence and disorders
at the Democratic Convention was roughly thirty-five years.
Is it not reasonable to wonder, therefore, whether the same
kind of chaos that befell Germany is now possible in the
United States in the decades ahead? Particularly in view of the
mounting violence, assassinations, and social disorder we have
experienced since the early 1960s.

More ominous still is the collapse of Liberalism in the
1960s and the rise of a New Left radicalism similar to that
which engulfed Europe prior to both World Wars. The concept of welfare statism and its underlying philosophical justification is a European import, via Britain: that is, via the
Fabian Socialists. The British Fabian Socialists borrowed
many of their Socialist ideas from the German Socialists of
the nineteenth century.

---

[144] *Ibid.*, pp. 164-65.

In the final analysis, the welfare state has been the bridgehead to the police state and dictatorship, for free representative government and democratic institutions cannot long coexist with either Socialism or its little sister, the welfare state. As Dr. Friedrich Hayck pointed out in his 1944 work, *The Road to Serfdom*, the only social system that makes democracy possible is Capitalism—which most Socialists would destroy, blindly assuming that democracy can survive with government controls.

As Dr. Hayek has written:

> We have progressively abandoned that freedom in economic affairs without which personal and political freedom has never existed in the past. . . .
> It is now often said that democracy will not tolerate "capitalism." If "capitalism" means here a competitive system based on free disposal over private property, it is far more important to realize that *only within this system is democracy possible.*[145] [My emphasis.]

The failure of sympathizers of welfare statism and Socialism to understand this important point has, in part, been the cause for much suffering in the earlier part of this century—suffering which Herbert Spencer foresaw so clearly as early as 1884. Today, we too have advance warning of what can follow—not only in violent events such as Chicago 1968, but in the works of such men as George Orwell, intellectual heir to Herbert Spencer, who gave us *1984*. It remains to be seen whether we shall be wiser in heeding Orwell and the warning he offers a still-free people, than was Europe in regard to Spencer in the late 1880s.

---

[145] *The Road to Serfdom* (The University of Chicago Press, 1944).

XV
The Root Source of the Attack on
Our Free Society

In the past the burden of taxation and bureaucratic incompetence built up to a point where the civilization collapsed, as in the case of the Roman Empire. That seems to be the way the story ends and we're headed that way. I don't mean our civilization will collapse tomorrow. It is a matter of time. I'd say about the year 2000, plus or minus.[146] [Stated in 1963 by C. Northcote Parkinson, British critic and author.]

The *Saturday Review* on March 22, 1969, reported that "in 1969 employed Americans will work two and a half hours every eight-hour working day to pay their tax bills—federal, state, and local."[147] Similar periodicals in recent times have spoken of a "taxpayers' revolt."

The welfare state in America has been growing for thirty-five years; if it continues at the same growth rate, America's development may very well parallel the forty-five years of welfare state policies in Germany from Bismarck to Hitler's takeover. But the years around 2000, when Parkinson predicts our civilization will collapse, constitute the era when today's college youth will be the "command generation," that is, will be of the age to be in positions of power and responsibility. (Today's command generation are the college graduates of the 1930s.)

The trend in the educational systems of America since the 1930s has been advocacy of Liberal and equalitarian policies promoting the welfare state. The college generation of the 1930s, graduates of this trend, helped elect John F. Kennedy and Lyndon Johnson, and influenced those who had not had the "benefit" of a college education. Kennedy's and Johnson's Administrations, in turn, managed to enact "New Frontier" and "Great Society" social legislations unprecedented in

---

[146] An Interview, *Associated Press* (September 12, 1963), reprinted in *World Telegram & Sun*.
[147] "Taxes—The Collection and Distribution of Your Money," *Saturday Review* (March 22, 1968).

scope since Roosevelt's New Deal. Today's college generation, influenced by radical professors carrying on the educational trend of the 1930s, will soon be in the position to
carry these same premises even farther.

This cycle of thought and action, if unchecked or unchallenged, can make Parkinson's prediction a nightmare reality.
Parkinson does not say it *will* happen; he says only that if the
current course of taxation and bureaucracy continues unchecked it is very possible that our civilization *could* collapse
under these burdens.

European history is a warning as to what can happen to a
nation that follows the unsound economic course America is
now pursuing. And to understand the present course of
America, and how we came to adopt the welfare state, it is
necessary to look back to the New Deal and the pervading
influences at the time.

The Seeds of Fabian Socialism

The philosophical and political fathers of Franklin D.
Roosevelt's New Deal were a small group of intellectuals who
began to organize in the growing power centers of nineteenth
century America—in education, in publishing, and in the
labor movement. Most of the ideas held by these intellectuals
were either Marxian Socialist or Populist. Another group,
known as Fabian Socialists, borrowed many of their ideas
from the British Fabians who were working to gain "social
control" through state power over the instruments of the
newly flowering Capitalist Industrial Revolution in England.

Although their ultimate aim was similar, the Fabians, unlike the Marxists, believed violent revolution was not necessary to seize the means of production. Borrowing the name
and the tactics employed by the Roman General Fabian Max-
imus against the Carthaginian hero, Hannibal—"attack . . . de-
lay . . . attack"—the Fabians postulated that through the
solar plexis of a free society (its educational system for example) the majority of citizens would come by peaceful means,
and in degrees, to accept Socialism. In America, however,
where individuality and freedom were highly prized, the Fabian Socialists thought it advisable to call themselves "progressives" and "liberals."

Thus, the New Deal was not born on Inauguration Day
1933, but at the turn of the century through the Capitalist-
supported centers of learning and commerce. As an example,

two intellectuals, historians Charles Beard, a Marxist, and
Frederick Jackson Turner, a Fabian Socialist, were enormous-
ly influential with their interpretations of American history
and their rewrites of many historical texts, which obscured
the monumental achievements of the American Industrial
Revolution. Beard imputed to the Founders of America evil
and mercenary motives for the creation of the U.S. Constitution. Turner insisted that with the end of the American frontier, individualism and with it free enterprise and entrepre-
neurship were finished. More important, Zygmund Dobbs in
his history of Socialism reveals that:

> Among those influenced by Turner was Franklin
> Delano Roosevelt, who absorbed his education in his-
> tory from Turner and Edward Channing. Channing was
> the son of Will Ellery Channing, well-known Fourierist
> Socialist advocate of a collectivist society.
> The future President of the United States, while bare-
> ly 20 years of age, was thus being taught [at Harvard]
> that the system of private enterprise had run its course,
> and that a controlled social order must take its place.
> *The germ of the New Deal was thus planted not in
> 1932, but soon after 1900.*[148] [My emphasis.]

Not only did the American "liberals" and "progressives"
borrow freely from the British Fabians, but patterned many
of their intellectual institutions after those in Britain. For
example, the New School (earlier known as the New School
for Social Research) was a direct copy of the London School
of Economics; the then future President of the United States,
John F. Kennedy, attended the London School while his
father was FDR's Ambassador to Britain in the 1930s.
Among the founders of New York's New School were Charles
Beard and educator-philosopher John Dewey. The education
theories of Dewey, a life-long Socialist, are still the most per-
vasive of those of any twentieth century intellectual. They
are accepted without question or examination—yet they are
largely the cause for the crisis in American education today.

The New Deal and "New Politics"

To illustrate the influence of American Fabians and Marxists of the New Deal on the current New Left, we need only
cite one principal character in this drama of the last four

---

[148] *The Great Deceit*, Veritas Foundation, West Sayville (New York,
1964), p. 73.

decades: Rexford G. Tugwell. He is by no means the only example, but his background will serve amply as illustration.

Tugwell was among FDR's "brain trusters" who vowed to "make America over."[149] FDR heeded Tugwell's philosophy. It was not entirely alien to him; he had learned of it from Frederick Jackson Turner at Harvard.

John T. Flynn in his work, *The Roosevelt Myth*, tells us that the man who most influenced Tugwell was a Marxian Socialist who was educated at Johns Hopkins and taught at Yale: Thorstein Veblen. He was one of the founders of the New School, and contributed his theories of "social economics" to the texts that were required reading for college students. Flynn says of Veblen:

> In an age when it was the popular thing in college to be in revolt, Veblen supplied his followers with a steady stream of alluring and half-baked slants on the world around them. The point that stuck with them was that our democratic system of business was run by a lot of ignoramuses and that the remedy was a new structure of society which the experts—the technicians and the professors—would take over. *This was government by elite, which is precisely what Mussolini believed in. . . .*[My emphasis.]
>
> One of the men who fell under the spell of this ribald and lawless iconoclast was Rex Tugwell and it was Tugwell, of all the men who had a chance to influence Roosevelt, who resembled Veblen most in the substance of his philosophy.[150]

Tugwell and his allies have made good, for three and a half decades, their pledge to "make America over." But instead of "planned Capitalism" the philosophy of the New Deal spawned "planned chaos." Now, in the late 1960s, Tugwell urges another generation of youth to finish what he and the supporters of FDR began in the 1930s.

In August 1967, for example, the Center for the Study of Democratic Institutions sponsored a New Left student radical seminar, attended by New Left campus leaders from across the nation. As a member of the symposium audience, Tugwell heard such statements as the following, made by the then student body president of Washington University in St. Louis, Devereaux Kennedy:

---

[149] John T. Flynn, *op. cit.*, p. 206.
[150] *Ibid.*, pp. 156-157.

People in universities can do a number of things. . . .
They can engage in acts of terrorism and sabotage outside the ghetto. But that's just a minor part of it. The
major thing student activists can do while all this is going on—I mean *completely demoralizing and castrating
America*—is to give people a vision other than what they
have now. . . .
What we have to do, first of all, is to define what we
think the enemy is. There's no doubt in my mind about
the enemy. It's monopoly Capitalism and imperialism.[151] [My emphasis.]

Later, Tugwell addressed the radicals and commented on
such remarks as the above, saying, "There will be a kind of
revolution, but it won't be the one you're talking about."[152]
(In the following chapter Tugwell spells out just what he
means, in his own words.)

Revolution—When a Nation Loses Its Nerve
It has puzzled many of the most respected Americans why
violence, like that in Chicago, should erupt in an era of unprecedented affluence and progress. The answer lies in the
fundamental weakness in the Liberal philosophy: its misconceptions about the nature of social reality. Violent events in
the 1960s are the direct result of Liberalism's revolt against
reason and reality; its premises will not sustain the weight of
reality closing in on all sides. As an example, the welfare system has drained many Negroes of self-esteem over the decades, keeping them in a dependent position, an economic
servitude, until finally an explosive social problem was created. In anger and frustration, blacks attacked Liberalism because of its hollowness and absence of moral standards. They
have been joined by white students who are revolting against
the hollow Liberal teachings in our universities. And Liberal
weakness continues to feed the New Left revolution with its
vacillating positions and shallow solutions. As C. Northcote
Parkinson observed:

In studying the history of revolt we find that it sel-
dom occurs, and still more rarely succeeds, under a regime
that is *sure of itself*. Our first mental picture may be of
brave men plotting against a crushing tyranny. . . . We

---
[151] *U.S.A. Magazine* (February 8, 1968).
[152] *Ibid.*

soon realize, however, that men are not as brave as that. They do not rebel against strength and cruelty, but *against weakness and indecision. Revolutions take place when the regime is wavering and, above all, divided.*[153] [My emphasis.]

America was founded and has flourished on principles of individualism, the philosophy of reason, and the protection of rights and liberty. Toward the end of the nineteenth century, Socialist intellectuals of America began a steady erosive campaign against these principles, climaxing in the counterrevolution of 1933 under FDR. Having operated on the principle that compulsion enforced by a few for the alleged good of the many will guarantee progress and social concord, America now is paying with the chaos we witness today. But instead of abandoning their unworkable premises, radicals of the New Left are urged on by power-seekers like Tugwell toward bringing full State Socialism to America. Chicago was only a warning of worse things to come.

Parkinson's observations about the bankruptcy of the British Fabians' programs might well apply to the Liberals in America and their New Left children:

> By 1949 the Labour Party had no single idea left, and it was at this moment that George Orwell published his book called *1984.* . . . For fifty years and more the Labour Party leaders had believed in the inevitability of progress. Their Social Democracy was bound to come and was certain to bring universal happiness. Readers of *1984* were suddenly made to realize that there is nothing inevitable about it. Socialism might not come at all and might prove—even should it come—a nightmare of injustice, oppression, and cruelty. Orwell, who had actually fought in Spain [during the Civil War of the 1930s] was left with no illusion about Progress. He could see, as could few other critics, that democracy was on the decline and that socialism, without democracy, means the end of freedom.[154]

The intellectuals in Europe in the earlier part of this century who espoused Socialism could not or would not recognize that the free market economy is the foundation for free democratic government; or that the rise of the power of the state and the decline of the free market leads ultimately, not

---

[153] *Left Luggage* (Houghton Mifflin Co.; Boston, 1967), p. 27.
[154] *Ibid.,* p. 133.

to Socialism, but to barbarism. The Weimar Republic, for example, vainly sought to make democratic government work in Germany after World War I while adopting more and more welfare state measures. Increasing state intervention in the economic life of the people later extended itself to the social and political arenas until National Socialism became totalitarian Nazism. ("Nazi" is an abbreviation for National Socialist German Workers' Party.)

One individual in our age who has recognized where Socialism eventually leads is the English author, John Braine (*Room at the Top*), who renounced Socialism in a revealing article in a pamphlet printed by a London conservative political society (later printed in the New York *Times* in March 1968). Braine made the connection between the principles of the free market and free democratic government during a trip to the United States—where, he records, his defection from Socialism was "total." The "key log," as he put it, was the concept of freedom. He wrote of his American visit:

Towards the end of the trip, I worked it out: the name of happiness was freedom. This was still a country in which one could be anything you wanted to be from beatnik to millionaire. This was a country in which still *the state existed for the people not the people for the state*. The name of the system the people lived under was capitalism. It was often cruel, often unjust, often inefficient, often wasteful, but it gave everyone, even in an arbitrary and confused way, the chance to be what he wanted to be. Above all, it didn't care. It left people alone. . . . *And, for all its faults, it gave the majority of people a far higher standard of living than did either Communism or its ugly little sister Socialism.*

There were pockets of devastating poverty but, given time, those would be wiped out. There was a racial problem alongside the poverty problem but, given time, that would be wiped out, too. The profit motive would do the job; *for what poverty represents to capitalism is not so much an evil as an untapped market.* [We would add, poverty is the *absence* of Capitalism.] The desire to make a profit out of one's fellow man is a more reliable and decent motive than the desire to do him good, to change his way of life to make him a better person.

For eventually he may find himself being made a better person in the torture chamber or the prison camp, or—for the good of the greatest number—on the gallows. The Capitalist sells him something which, by and large, has to be reasonable value for money if he wants to make another sale. But he doesn't care what the customer believes or what color he is as long as he gets his money.... The richest man in the U.S.A. has not the power of life and death. The most minor bureaucrat in the Soviet Secret Police can exercise it a hundred times a day.[155] [My emphasis.]

Perhaps as Braine had introduced Socialism to his friend Orwell, the latter had planted seeds of doubt about that philosophy; and the hope of individual freedom—not just for himself, but for all men—was concretized by the freedom Braine found in the United States.

We know the underlying reasons why John Braine renounced his old political faith for freedom. But Prince Philip gives us a concrete illustration to validate Braine's abstract arguments. Life under British Socialism, with its compulsion to plan the lives of its people, is captured in the comments of Queen Elizabeth's consort:

> LONDON (AP)—Prince Philip fired another broadside at Britain today, asserting that far too many people were "just sitting around," others were smothered by government controls, and the truly creative were inadequately rewarded.
>
> The 47-year-old husband of Queen Elizabeth made his comments in an interview with the Director, a magazine for business executives. It followed a recent TV interview in which the Prince said Britons now-a-days practically *need a license to breathe.*
>
> Citing an experience on the royal family's estate in Scotland, Prince Philip said:
>
> "We had to get planning permission to block up a fireplace in a cottage. Really it's unbelievable. There are controls saying you can't build a woodshed nearer than 25 feet to the back door of a cottage.
>
> *"Over everything you try to do there is a control or sanction.* I think the worst is that you can't take more than 50 pounds ($120) abroad."
>
> Prince Philip conceded the British might have brought controls on themselves *"because instead of people being self-disciplined they are determined to take advantage of the system."*[156] [My emphasis.]

---

[155] John Braine, "Why One British Socialist Turned Conservative," *The New York Times Magazine* (March 2, 1969).
[156] New York *Post* (March 5, 1969)

XVI
The Totalitarian Mr. Tugwell—Beyond 1984, to the Year 2000

We are different from all the oligarchies of the past in that we know what we are doing. [O'Brien the Inquisitor states in Orwell's *1984*] They pretended, perhaps they even believed, that they had seized power unwillingly and for a limited time. And that just around the corner there lay a paradise where human beings would be free and equal. We are not like that. We know that no one seizes power with the intention of relinquishing it. Power is not a means; it is an end. One does not establish a dictatorship in order to safeguard a revolution; *one makes the revolution in order to establish the dictatorship. The object of persecution is persecution. The object of torture is torture. The object of power is power.*[157] [My emphasis.]

George Orwell's genius as the most persuasive critic of a totalitarian order grew from the fact that, as a former Fabian Socialist, he profoundly understood the *consequence of ideas*. His nightmarish novel, *1984*, is a warning of what can happen to a society if it renounces reason, critical independent thought, and individuality to a collectivist creed. It is apparent that Orwell understood that such a nightmare was possible if the cultural and intellectual trends he observed prior to and after World War II continued unchallenged and unchecked.

And it is now possible to state categorically that there are men and women in the West, and in America particularly, who possess the totalitarian mentality and philosophy to make Orwell's fictional, Big Brother, total collectivist state a living reality.

The Totalitarian Braintrusters
Ever since the advent of the New Deal, the Americans for Democratic Action (ADA) have acted as the intellectual "think tank" for the Democratic Party. In the 1960s, however, a more radical leftist organization has slowly supplanted

---

[157] *1984* (New York; New American Library, 1961), p. 219.

the ADA: The Center for the Study of Democratic Institutions. Besides creating the National Conference for New Politics in 1965 and various seminars for "peace" and "social change" (meaning change to a Socialist order), The Center has played host to such aspiring political figures as Senator Edward Kennedy. In fact, during a 1969 speech at The Center, Kennedy proposed the seating of Red China and its National antagonist in the U.N., and a *"rapprochement"* between the U.S. and Red China—a major policy position of The Center.[158]

The Center's activity in the political arena is carried on despite the clear violation of its status as a tax-exempt foundation. (The law forbids that tax-exempt foundations engage in political activity. However, The Center, we should add, is not alone in violating this statute.)[159]

One of the long-range projects of The Center is the creation of a "new constitution," that will guarantee social and economic rights—not individual or political rights. The Presidential assistant and speech writer for John F. Kennedy, Theodore Sorenson, is on record as favoring such a "new constitution"; Sorenson, today, is major advisor to Senator Ted Kennedy.

One of FDR's brain trusters, and now a member of The Center, Rexford Tugwell, has confessed that most of the welfare state legislation enacted during the New Deal was *in violation of the Constitution of 1789*, although at the time it was said to be in concert with that document. Tugwell made these admissions in advocating a "new constitution" consistent with his Socialist bias. Tugwell further contends, rightly, that the Constitution was a "negative document" which *protected the rights of its citizens*, but in no way charged the government for looking after the economic welfare o its citizens.

What Tugwell meant, when he told a gathering of radical New Left student leaders at The Center in August 1967 that "there will be a kind of revolution but it won't be the one you're talking about," he spelled out in a November 1968 article titled, "U.S.A. 2000 A.D." In effect, Tugwell speculated on what the United States would be like in the year

[158] *U.S. News & World Report* (February 24, 1968).
[159] Publisher Alice Widener reported in *U.S.A. Magazine* (August, 1967) that "The Center" is the sole institution supported by the Fund for the Republic, which was created in 1954 by a $15,000,000 grant from the Ford Foundation.

2000. Writing as if he were a historian looking back on the latter half of the twentieth century, his article reads like George Orwell's *1984*.

Tugwell's Totalitarian Tomorrow

"As political entities," Tugwell wrote of the individual states of the American union, "they had been submerged in the mighty sweep of social and economic integration following the technological developments of the sixties and seventies.[160]

The Center has long advocated that the States of the Union were "anachronisms" and that local and state governments should be abolished altogether. But this compulsion for "centralization" of power, of Tugwell and other totalitarian intellectuals of the Left, could also be observed in his view of the States of the World. Tugwell—as the historian of the year 2000—wrote from the high imaginary perch of perspective:

> Like the states, nations might be in their last stages, but they continued to insist on independence. Nevertheless, the conditions requiring integration were overcoming opposition in the same way it had been overcome when *states and provincial politicians had tried to assert their independence.*[161] [My emphasis.]

While not openly stated, the use of force is implied to compel those nations to see the world as one state for mankind. This is consistent with the fact that Tugwell and other brain trusters in the New Deal sold Franklin Roosevelt on the idea of the United Nations. Tugwell's "one-world order" with its underlying philosophical premises of Fabian Socialism is not so mythical—since the same feature has dominated the U.N. since its founding.

As to Capitalism of the future, Tugwell tells us from the year 2000:

> It was not until the seventies that *industrial regulation became effective.* . . . They [speaking of the corporate conglomerates that were forced into mergers in the 1960s by the FDR New Deal maze of regulatory agencies and repressive taxation] could even buy other businesses with the excuse of diversification. They became

---

[160] Rexford G. Tugwell "U.S.A. 2000 A.D.," *The Center Magazine* (November 1968). Published by The Center for the Study of Democratic Institutions, Santa Barbara, California.

[161] *Ibid.*

empires and controls of them grew so centralized that, lacking any standards of fairness, the strong became more and more effective in exploiting the weak. . . .

[However] . . . industries had begun to reach more rational arrangements among themselves simply because they had to. This had not happened, however, *until the government had consented to bring them into a loose confederation and had established standards of fairness. The precedent in 1933 of the National Recovery Administration, abandoned because of the hostility of the influential atomists, was useful for the purpose.*[162] [My emphasis.]

Clearly Tugwell is talking about extended government control of the "means of production."

He writes as if the events of the last half of this century—with all its force, compulsion, and dictation by an intellectual elitist government—were carried forth by forces which rational men could not hope to oppose. The enforcement of those "rational arrangements" between industry and government were, from Tugwell's totalitarian view, brought about by the club of government compulsion. As to "standards of fairness," this is another nineteenth and twentieth century bromide peddled by the "New Marxists" or the Old Left. What is fair to one individual or business, may not be fair to another. This fact of life was largely responsible for the collapse of the National Recovery Administration (NRA) in the Roosevelt era—which Tugwell and his intellectual elitists at The Center would reintroduce into American economic life. No less a totalitarian tomorrow, from Tugwell's viewpoint, is his observation from the year 2000 that labor relations had reached such a state that "compulsory arbitration was resorted to. . . ." And as for the wage earner in the second half of the twentieth century, it is clear that an increasing portion of his earnings is to be confiscated by the government.

Mind Control in America

"It was naturally an awesome thought," Tugwell tells us, *"that, by manipulation, human natures could be altered*; and there had been those who felt strongly that even if such knowledge existed it ought to be locked away out of sight. But this had never yet been done successfully with any

---

[162] *Ibid.*

scientific discovery. *Personalities were being altered.*"[163] [My emphasis.]

Sounding like the Nazi advocates of race supremacy he continues his insidious assertion that personality manipulation and mind control would be a fact of the future. He adds:

> As far back as the early days of the century there had been talk of a super-race whose individuals would behave toward each other with restraint and would join in advancing civilization. The World Wars had shown that these hopes were premature. Anyway, scientists had been delayed in discovering ways to influence human behaviour. *Now these were becoming known and what remained was to adopt public policy for their use. Identification of the chemical and electrical impulses of bodily adjustments was now well advanced.*[164] [My emphasis.]

However insidious this may seem, what Tugwell is expressing, although he claims that the article is only "speculation," is the extension of certain premises that have been carried forth since the New Deal. As one of the architects of the New Deal, Tugwell and others put into practice, on an unprecedented scale in American society, the philosophy that it was morally proper for the government to use force (regulations enforced by law) to compel its citizens to accept certain policies allegedly for their own good. This premise, set into motion by FDR, grew in the Truman, Eisenhower, Kennedy, Johnson, and now Nixon Administrations. The intellectual hoodlums inside and outside the Democratic Convention in August 1968, as well as the activists in the early civil rights movement, carried this principle from the Government into the streets—believing that it was morally proper to use force to achieve political objectives. Now, if we follow Tugwell's and The Center's plan for the future, this principle of compulsion will be carried even into the area of mind and personality control—all for the individual's "good" and for that of the collective whole.

The Fascists, Nazis, and Communists, at least in their early stages of coming to power, enunciated this same premise of control for everyone's good. Their climaxes have been hideous nightmares. But Tugwell's support of such ideas is not surprising. Other Socialists in the early days of totalitarianism

---

[163] *Ibid.*
[164] *Ibid.*

in their respective countries (Russia, Germany, Italy, and other smaller countries), applauded and welcomed their totalitarian regimes. They found it politically and socially expedient to recognize them publicly as barbaric only after their "noble social experiments" produced the slaughter of millions in death camps or systematic campaigns of starvation and extermination.

Individualism: Barrier Against Barbarism

The critical feature which made all the collectivist tyrannies of the twentieth century possible was the constant advocacy by philosophers, intellectuals, and religious leaders that the individual must surrender his sovereignty to the collective whole or to the collective good. Tugwell and other totalitarians have preached this ethic since the days of the New Deal, and today they are prepared to use the "surrender of individual sovereignty" of millions for their own power purposes. As Tugwell tells us:

> People must give up thinking only of themselves—how they can increase their pleasures, how they can make certain of their incomes. . . . the rule of laissez-faire must be abandoned. *Individuals following their own interests do not contribute to the good of the whole. The rule must read that every man, guided by the interest of the whole and contributing to it, will find his own well-being increased by the general product*—it can be increased in no other way. . . .[165] [My emphasis.]

The intellectual and moral dishonesty of the above cannot be overstated. In effect, Tugwell presents us with an impossible contradiction: that individuals must renounce their own self-interest in their own self-interest! But who, in Tugwell's frame of reference, is to decide what is one group's self-interest and not another's? Who is to be that impartial agent of decision? Having once renounced one's individuality for the collective whole, the only agent would of course be the Government:

> As for the government, if it was to be recognized as *the agent of the people* instead of their potential enemy, it must be organized to do what was required of it [required by whom and for what end? Ed.] rather than prevented from taking any action because it might seem

---

[165] *Ibid.*

to favor some over others. *The balance of powers and checking devised for the protection of the individual must be modified to encourage forward movement.*[166] [My emphasis.]

"Forward movement" to what end is not spelled out in this projection of social affairs. But to make all this "legal," Tugwell would enact a "new constitution" that "must be adopted to this principle"—meaning to collectivism. As for the individual's protection from tyranny and the evils of men in power, Tugwell states that *"the right of the individual to protection from oppression must be matched with a duty to participate."*

In other words, the individual who now, under the "old" Constitution is guaranteed the right of life, liberty, freedom of speech, and freedom of choice in political affairs, would be guaranteed such rights only if he *participates* in the society.

All of these features are frighteningly similar to what Orwell warned about in his novel, *1984*. While they were contained in a fictional context, Tugwell and his colleagues at The Center would—knowingly or unconsciously—make them a reality. And it has already been demonstrated that to sell these manifestly totalitarian ideas to other intellectuals, political, and moral leaders in America, they must be advertised in the name of freedom, peace, harmony, and security.

The people of America will come to accept the Tugwell vision of tomorrow so long as they are uncertain and confused as to the principles and philosophy required to wage a battle against it. And until such a battle is waged the neobarbarism which has beset America in the second half of this century will thrive.

XVII
Do We Need a Modern Manifesto for Our Troubled Times?

Machiavelli contends that states are easily corrupted by the passing of time. (We say they age.) To save them from death, it is necessary to urge them to return to "their first principles" so that they can generate the same vitality and youthfulness they had at the start.[167] [Professor Giuseppe Prezzolini wrote of the fifteenth century Florentine diplomat whose name has become synonymous with duplicity.]

It will startle some Americans to discover that at least three of America's Founding Fathers—John Jay, Benjamin Franklin, and John Adams—drew upon the works of Machiavelli in their fight for American independence from the British crown. John Adams, for example, looked to Machiavelli's *Florentine Histories* as the basis for his own work, "A Defense of the Constitutions of Government of the United States."

The current crisis confronting America today requires that we seriously consider Machiavelli's advice that if a nation is to save itself from death, it must return to the "first principles" and philosophy which gave it life and liberty. In the case of America, these are the principles and philosophy concretized in the Declaration of Independence and the United States Constitution.

Can a People Live in the Past?

Considerable confusion and distortion has dominated the thinking of Americans in regard to those concepts and ideas upon which the American system was founded. One distortion is the belief that the U.S. Constitution is a "relic" of the past and therefore unresponsive to the problems of the twentieth century. Another glib charge promoted by many Liberals is that those who insist upon a fidelity to the principles and philosophy of 1776 and 1789 are somehow "living in the past," and that eighteenth or nineteenth century thinking will not solve twentieth century problems. These arguments have never been fully analyzed or effectively refuted.

---

[167] *Machiavelli* (New York; Farrar, Strauss & Giroux, 1967).

On all sides there is a gross ignorance of the fact that every century has had a direct influence, usually profound, on the succeeding century. Today's technological achievements, for example, are the direct result of the mechanical inventions and achievements of the nineteenth century; and those were made possible, in part, by the kind of social system the Founding Fathers of America created in the latter eighteenth century. Without the past, the present—with all its comforts and benefits—could not be.

Americans of the second half of this century certainly cannot go back to 1776. What we can and must do, if we are to meet the challenges and overcome the real dangers that confront the American system for the remaining decades of this century, is to fashion a manifesto based on sound principles. It is the *absence* of a sound set of principles in the dominant Liberal philosophy which is the cause for the turmoil and unrest in the 1960s—and which led us to the tragic events (active and responsive) at the 1968 Democratic Convention in Chicago.

New York University Professor William Buckler has suggested that the crisis in American universities in particular and in the nation in general "opens up a dialogue that has largely been closed for sixty-five years; a dialogue on alternative ideas as expressed by John Locke, the Founding Fathers, Cardinal Newman, and others."[168]

In other words, Professor Buckler insists Americans need to consider that the alternative to the dominant Liberal philosophy (although he did not use the term) may be found in those principles and philosophy which modern Americans have largely discarded or ignored.

Far from "going back," we need to "rediscover" the principles which were responsible for America's unprecedented material and social progress. It is these very principles and premises that comprise an alternative to what Liberalism has offered as a blueprint for our national future.

We Need Intellectual Weapons

"The problem in 1968," wrote author John Dos Passos, "is whether we can improvise a workable program . . . fast enough to reverse the trend towards disintegration and anarchy. . . .

---

[168] Dr. William E. Buckler, "Sunrise Semester," lecture, WCBS-TV (New York, March 24, 1969).

"The time for generalities is past. Someone must present a practical chart for the future which will restore to the American people a sense of direction."[169]

This program, however, will not succeed if it is comprised of slogans and catch phrases; it must contain an intelligent, consistent, and meaningful set of principles. Americans of reason and good will can never hope to cope with the violence and unrest that modern Liberalism has created, and forestall an Orwellian nightmare in the future, if their opposition is founded on premises of negation and shrill despair.

We must "rediscover" those principles propounded by a mere minority of men in 1776, and we must complete the American Revolution. The American Revolution was interrupted; we have yet to carry consistently the principles of 1776 and 1789 to their ends. Individualism, reason, liberty, and law must be applied to individual as well as national problems. But first we must recognize why and how the course of our nation was interrupted, and how we can return to it.

Americans cannot hope to challenge modern Liberalism and its New Left allies effectively unless we have intellectual weapons—full understanding of and the consequent confidence in the principles of a free republic. Our most substantial and meaningful point of reference for these principles is rooted in the *classic liberal* tradition—characterized by the philosophy of reason and individualism and manifestly set against the encroachment of individual rights by the power of the State. The problem is how to apply these principles to the present and to the future.

First, however, non-Liberals must divest themselves of certain misconceptions that have been the principal cause for their ineffectiveness in challenging Liberalism since FDR's New Deal.

The Weak and Reedy Voice of the Right

The violence at the Democratic Convention and the disorders of the 1960s in our nation's cities and on our college campuses can rightly be laid at the door of Liberalism. But at the same time, Liberalism's success until Chicago must also be attributed to the failure of the American Right.

The failure of concerned Conservatives, responsible Republicans, and classic liberals is vividly illustrated, for example, in

---

[169] John Dos Passos, *National Review* (August 13, 1968).

our colleges. In 1960 the Conservative-oriented student organization, Young Americans for Freedom (YAF), was originated under the leadership of *National Review* editor and Conservative spokesman William F. Buckley, Jr. In 1962, Students for a Democratic Society (SDS) began a campaign to capture the loyalty of American college youth, dressing up its philosophy of Socialism as something "new." Almost a decade later, while yet a campus minority, SDS wields substantial influence; and it has been the principal moving force in mounting a radical and violent assault on American institutions. YAF, in contrast, has failed to attract a sizable student and young adult following, and has failed to respond to the irrationality of the SDS's verbal, physical, and property destruction; even by many students who have no love for the SDS, YAF is regarded as an intellectual joke.

YAF's failure to command a broad-based following, or even to rally the "uncommitted" to its point of view, is a contemporary illustration of a long-standing weakness in Conservatives. Their ineffectiveness suggests the absence of a firm philosophical base. A consistent philosophical context provides an individual a standard by which to judge ideas, to discriminate between good and bad ideas, and thus to formulate consistent, logical alternatives to what, for instance, the New Left and SDS are proposing and effecting.

YAF's inability to refute effectively the SDS claims of "rights" and "morality" suggests that its members and adult leadership do not really understand the meaning of the American Revolution or of the free market system, which they say they support. Their inability to articulate intelligently the positive virtues of the very system which SDS is attacking leaves YAF members disarmed and unable to answer New Left distortions and smears, which later will be accepted as truths by a majority of students, who have not been exposed to a clear alternative. Any smear or distortion of fact will stick if promulgated long enough and loudly enough and if not met with intelligent opposition.

This same set of criticisms can be made of many adults who say they are opposed to modern Liberalism and the New Left. Since FDR's New Deal, adult Conservatives have floundered in a sea of emotions and contradictions brought about by an imprecise and unclear understanding of Liberalism as a philosophy, and of the ultimate social and political consequences of that philosophy. And at the same time they propose pot-shot alternatives to what Liberalism offers.

Why the Lost Ground to Liberalism

It is the major mistake of Conservatives and Republicans that they have always allowed Liberals to set the terms of the battle. The Republicans, especially, have too often expressed themselves by means of "me-tooism." Not understanding the full import of Liberal proposals such as Medicare, and accepting the Liberal's definition of the problem, Republicans and Conservatives acknowledge that such a program is "needed." But, in the case of Medicare, *was* it needed? And if so, needed at what expense to our social system and to the individual? A lower quality of medical care and an increased burden of involuntary taxation on the individual is a high price. Did non-Liberals consider the logical conclusion of the Medicare proposal—that Medicare is only part of a long-range Liberal program for legislating more radical approaches to social policy? Pandora's box was opened under the Republican Eisenhower Administration with the token medical aid measure (for the extremely poor) of the Kerr-Mills bill. Out flew Medicare under the later Administration of Lyndon Baines Johnson. Today the New Left and its radical organization, Medical Committee for Human Rights, is seeking to push the enactment of a U.S. National Health Service! Not really, we should add, to improve health care, but as part and parcel of a long-range aim of destroying private medicine in America: they advocate that private medical treatment is inadequate and thus all aspects of medicine should be run by the State.

The disastrous National Health Service in Socialist Britain offers America a stern warning; nor should we overlook the concurrent widespread policy of State control which is shattering Britain's economy and stifling all individuality, inventiveness, industrial creativity, and medical advances. Yet arguments against Medicare were raised in a weak and inarticulate fashion, or not at all.

Medicare is not an isolated example; the foregoing points can be applied to almost all areas of U.S. social and economic life toward which Liberalism has aimed its ideological gunsights. For instance, welfare assistance is regarded by many as essential. Yet it has provided the wedge for Liberals and the New Left radicals to push for federal control—and for its ugly step-sister, the national guaranteed income.

Conservatives have failed to emphasize the salient fact that Liberalist proposals are designed for the destruction of liberty; compulsion, greater and greater federal controls, and correspondingly less freedom cannot help but lead to something similar to the hideous nightmare that engulfed the German people. That America is already moving in that direction is illustrated by the fact that Liberals are willing to accommodate themselves to the more radical New Left—the sheep of social concern are now donning the robes of the rapacious wolves.

The Conservative has an overwhelming advantage when he understands the roots of his deepest-held convictions and philosophy. And when he can differentiate between Socialism that parades under the banner of Liberalism and classic liberalism with its roots in the principles and concrete events set forth in 1776.

Liberalism as a Counterrevolution

Conservatives have never effectively exposed to Americans what modern Liberalism really is: European and British in origin and a counterrevolutionary movement against individualism, limited government, and individual rights. Any serious and consistent examination of Liberalism reveals a philosophy and principles just opposite to those enunciated by the Founders. Since the New Deal, Liberalism has been left to grow on the false assertion that its actions in matters of public policy were in the spirit of the American Revolution.

Liberalism espouses psychological collectivism, state control or unlimited government, and collective rights (with the individual reduced to a common denominator).

We are in reality confronted with a crucial and historic struggle between the philosophies underlying two revolutions: the 1776 Revolution of rights, freedom, and limited government; and the 1933 counterrevolution of growing government compulsion in violation of individual rights. Stripped of its slogans, nihilism, and irrational arguments, today's New Left is not only seeking to go beyond FDR's counterrevolution, but is seeking the complete destruction of, the philosophy of 1776.

The current dangers to individual freedom and security have developed due to the absence of an intelligent opposition to Liberalism rather than to the strengths of its philosophy. Had Liberalism been faced with an intelligent and consistent alternative philosophy earlier in the twentieth century it would have collapsed long ago, rather than in the 1960s sinking under the sheer weight of its own defects.

The Liberal welfare state came by degrees, not by any overwhelming endorsement by the majority of Americans. They simply accepted what was offered because they were never given an alternative philosophy of clear principles, which pinpointed the dangerous consequences of Liberalism. Today the New Left wants to go beyond the welfare state. It can only succeed if left unchallenged; so that Americans are left to accept today's irrational New Left nostrums as tomorrow's political dogma—by degrees, by propaganda, and by default.

The only philosophy that can effectively wage the battle against New Left Liberalism is that which produced the most productive and free social system in the history of mankind: the philosophy and principles enunciated by the Founding Fathers. By "rediscovering" the American Revolution and seeking to complete the goals of the Founders, we will find that we *have* an affirmative "manifesto" for our troubled times.

XVIII
Gunpowder Patriots and the American Military Tradition

There is nothing more common than to confound the terms of the American Revolution with those of the late American war. The American war is over, but this is far from being the case with the American Revolution. On the contrary, nothing but the first act of a great drama is closed. . . . We have changed our forms of government, but it remains yet to effect a revolution of our principles, opinions, and manners so as to accommodate them to the forms of government we have adopted."[170] [Dr. Benjamin Rush, a signer of the Declaration of Independence.]

Have we, almost twenty decades after the signing of the Declaration of Independence, continued to confound the terms of the American Revolution with the War for Independence? Has an emphasis on the military aspects of American history distorted the real moral meaning of our traditions, thus leaving the nation disarmed in the face of the violent attacks on its institutions, such as we saw at the Democratic Convention in Chicago, August 1968?

The answers to these questions are crucial in view of the weak opposition offered by classic liberals and Conservatives in the face of the onslaught of modern Liberalism. Conservatives, perhaps more than classic liberals, have tended to project our history in military terms. A couple of notable examples from among many: The traditional citation is the valor and courage of the men at Valley Forge. Their courage is unquestionable, but the philosophical and political goals of that battle are obscured. Valley Forge was but a military instrument for achieving those goals. We have memorialized in Lincoln's Gettysburg Address the price in lives the Union armies paid; but left unsung is the Civil War's profound influence in changing the direction of our nation, and in erasing a moral compromise committed by the Founders—their refusal to abolish slavery.

---

[170] Merrill Jensen, *Founding of a Nation* (New York; Oxford University Press, 1968), p. xi.

It is this undue emphasis on the military aspects of American history by many sincere individuals that has robbed them of legitimate intellectual weapons with which to oppose Liberalism in this century. When a nation's institutions are under attack, as are America's today, the manner of response by those who say they cherish such institutions is critically important. If these attacks go unanswered, if the answers are riddled with contradictions, the charges leveled against such institutions seem more credible. If responses are emotional (no matter how well intended), the more thoughtful individual—and particularly youth who are searching for reasoned answers—remains unconvinced, and uncertain. Meanwhile Liberals will continue to exploit and distort the American past for their own power purposes.

The Gunpowder Patriot and the New Generation

The emphasis on the military tradition of America in a type of *gunpowder patriotism* has unintentionally turned off American youth to the true American tradition and those principles which produced our greatness as a nation; and has left them defenseless in the face of attacks on the Constitution, individual rights, and the free economic system. This emphasis may, in fact, be the root source for so many young people regarding "patriotism" as corny or old-fashioned.

Much more serious, this failure of youth to answer the attacks on the nation and its institutions gives an advantage to the violent New Left in their intent to undermine and destroy America's institutions. If young people are bereft of the intellectual and moral ammunition to answer, such attacks tend to gain the appearance of legitimacy with the passing of time.

It is important to understand two things about the New Left and its success on the college campuses of the country. First, its victories have largely been victories by default because of the absence of an intelligent, consistent, and articulate opposition. Most students are unable to answer such distortions as the claim that this is a racist or sick society, or to point out the contradictions inherent in such statements. For example, how is it possible to prove that an entire society is racist? What measurement or yardstick do you use?

Second, the New Left *seems* to be addressing itself to our nation's problems in moral and philosophical terms.

Young people, in all ages of history, have been in search of
moral and philosophical answers to life's problems; a con-
stellation of principles that can help them navigate through
life. Perhaps no generation in our nation's history has been
more eager, even desperate, to understand the moral and philosophical meaning of America than today's youth. Young
people know—whether or not they can name it—that the current state of America, not completely free and not completely controlled by government, is a contradiction. The confusion we see in today's youth is which to choose: the philosophy of the freedom of the Founders or the philosophy of
force of government. The young sense, too, that the Founding Fathers stood four square for individuals controlling their
own lives in a responsible way; the most frequently heard
complaint of the young is that they do not have control over
their lives.

The New Left seems to offer such a philosophy, when in
reality the solutions they would enact would mean less, not
more, individual control of one's life. Highly emotional in
their youth, college students fail to examine this contradiction of the New Left. If Americans would give young people
one reasoned argument for the philosophy of individualism,
reason, and rights of the Founding Fathers, in an intelligent
and consistent fashion, it would undercut the effectiveness of
the New Left. Instead, what young people are offered, in
urging them to love their country and revere its traditions
and institutions, are vague generalities and a summons to
faith without reasons. The New Left, while offering wrong
reasons for its actions, does in fact formulate its case in what
appear to be specific grievances.

The Founders of America formulated their case for the
establishment of our system of government on solid grounds
of reason, moral principle, and its practical application to ensure freedom. The Founders, too, addressed themselves to
men's heads and their hearts. When the meaning of America
is expressed to the youth in terms of military gunpowder
patriotism, that meaning is lost to them. This is not to diminish the unquestionable valor of our military heroes in time of
war; but what is often overlooked is the emphasis on the individual character, devotion to a moral code, and to the cause
of individual liberty and peace.

The military draft laws constitute a searing illustration of
the failure, and even damage, caused by gunpowder patri-

otism. When we emphasize America's military tradition and victories as the reasons young Americans should love their country, and serve it, we too often omit the meaning behind this tradition. The use of force to obtain such service, despite the lack of love or reason, breeds in youth resentment rather than love of country; and denies in action the very principles that could bring a rebirth of the youthful patriotism we long to see.

Children respond to heroic tradition because they sense meaning behind it; as they grow older they crave identification and definition of this meaning; to the extent they can't find it, the response dies. The meaning they seek, and we omit, lies in the principles that made freedom and material progress in America possible, principles embodied in the Declaration of Independence and the U.S. Constitution, principles our Founding Fathers knew to be worth fighting for. It was the remaining sense of these principles, not as clearly defined, in defense of which men and women enlisted in World Wars I and II.

But the sense of such principles deteriorates without definition, and contradictions become more blatant. We cannot expect the young to support a system that seems to violate its founding charter in actions contrary to its principles; it is the very integrity of youth that makes even an unconscious hypocrisy of this sort unforgivable in their eyes.

The issue of the draft and its clear contradiction to the U.S. Constitution is used by the New Left, not constructively —such as to urge the replacement of conscription with a competitively salaried volunteer army—but to gain wide student support for its political program of destruction and violence. They use this needless contradiction to indict the entire society as militarist and corrupt. Repetition of these charges over the years, largely unchallenged and unrefuted, has produced a certain credibility for the New Left's additional charge that business profits from defense are the cause of wars like Vietnam. Unable to defend their own country against such fallacious and unfounded smears, most students who do love America, but are not sure why, respond with silence.

Our Legacy of Life, Liberty, Happiness

Little emphasis is given in our high schools and colleges today to the fact that the American Revolution was founded on a profound and, at that time, revolutionary premise—that each individual has a right to life, liberty, and the pursuit of happiness. This means *his* life, *his* liberty, and *his* pursuit of happiness; and it means that no other individual, no state, and no government, has a moral claim on those rights. The Founding Fathers specifically spelled out that ours was a government charged with the moral duty to protect these rights, a government strictly limited in its power to force or compel an individual to act against his will. The Declaration of Independence and later the U.S. Constitution clearly embody this concept.

Today the military conscription laws are in profound contradiction to the Founders' philosophy, to the Declaration of Independence, and to the United States Constitution. College students recognize this through their study (however inadequate) of American history, and regard those adults who support the draft as hypocrites. The majority of young people cannot find validity in such contradictions—and they reluctantly concur with the New Left that the American system is a fraud and a hoax.

Despite inconsistencies and contradictions in the arguments of the New Left, in their appeals to youth relative to the draft issue and war, they touch upon the primary interest of youth seeking individuality—self. The contiguous issues exploited by the New Left merely confirm for many young Americans the contradictions in our system.

Much to his credit, President Richard M. Nixon, in one of his first acts on taking office, set forth a proposal to correct the serious, potentially lethal constitutional contradiction and conflict inherent in the draft laws: he urged Congress to abolish the draft and replace it with a Volunteer Army. It is curious that certain political and intellectual leaders continue to support retention of the draft. It is especially curious that two such leaders are political "peace candidates," Senators Edward M. Kennedy of Massachusetts and Eugene McCarthy of Minnesota—both of whom claim to speak for the nation's youth.

The New Left says it speaks for the nation's youth, too, and it has persistently condemned the draft—yet it refuses to support President Nixon's proposal for abolition of the draft. In addition to its inherent contradiction, this position negates totally the New Left's claim that its active advocacy of violence is based on the moral example of the Founding Fathers. The Founders explicitly advocated that no society can remain free if an individual or group of individuals is allowed to use physical force to achieve political objectives—or to *initiate* physical force for any objective whatever.

Many adult Americans insist that the draft is a necessity for national defense. But at what price? For if that price is the progressive loss of youthful loyalty to the American system of government—and exploitation by the New Left—then perhaps this is far too high a price to pay when alternatives have been proposed.

The American political leadership's conduct of the Vietnam war provides another blatant contradiction that the New Left uses for its own power purposes. Young men are expected to fight, in the face of possible maiming or even death, in a war that seems to make no sense. While we are offering inconsistent justification for waging such a war, which we announced in its early stages we did not seek to win, young men in the jungles hear from Radio Hanoi that it is the *North Vietnamese* goal to seek victory over "American Imperalism." This obvious contradiction is only an extension of the contradictions on our domestic policy.

Therefore, it is not difficult to understand that when many young Americans hear and see the American tradition projected in military or gunpowder patriotic terms they tune out and turn off. Matters are not helped any when biased intellectuals and professors project the American tradition in distorted and evil terms—a past allegedly characterized by slavery, brutality, and oppression.

The Dark Heart of U.S. History?

We began after all as a people who killed red men and enslaved black people . . . but no nation, however righteous its professions, could act as we did without burying deep in itself, in its institutions, and its psyche a propensity toward violence.

Nor do we confine our violence to red and black men. We gained our independence, after all, through revolution. The first century after independence were years of incessant violence, wars, slave insurrections, Indian fighting, urban rioting, murders, duels and beatings. . . .[171]
[Liberal historian Arthur Schlesinger, Jr.]

This distorted one-sided portrait of the American past is widespread in the nation's colleges. These events did take

---

[171] "The Dark Heart of History," *Saturday Review* (October 19, 1968).

place, but to present such a selective and tailored view of the American past, ignoring its crucially important affirmative achievements, is both intellectually dishonest and morally reprehensible. Most historians like Schlesinger have become "prosecutors of the past"—with the calculated aim of erasing from the minds of Americans the principles and the philosophy which made America great. It is, as Harvard historian and Professor Samuel Eliot Morison termed, "the American intellectual revolt against our country and history." Historians who display selective views look longingly toward Europe and the Socialist tradition; or they look to such historical Americans as Andrew Jackson, whom Schlesinger admires and has written about. But Jackson was the first of a long line of Presidents who expressed a collectivist, rather than an individualist, philosophy. Although Jackson himself was very much a rugged individualist, he did not apply that philosophy to the Presidential Administration of our Government.

Biased historians bridle at the fact that the majority of American people still adhere to the philosophy of individualism; they and their predecessors have tried for more than a century now to discredit the true and affirmative American tradition, projecting it in the most violent and evil terms—whether it be in imputing unsavory motives to the framers of the U.S. Constitution, as did Socialist historian Charles Beard, or claiming that the nineteenth century was characterized by plunder and oppression by money-hungry and power-greedy men of the Capitalist classes.

Acts of violence in the past must be emphasized to discredit the whole past, so that Americans will seek so-called "new" progressive answers to our mounting problems. These progressive answers will allegedly purify the dark heart of history by scrapping such "anachronisms" as the U.S. Constitution of 1789, in favor of a "social constitution." But this pat answer, this selective view of the past, does not square with the facts. Affirmative achievements were taking place during that period which Schlesinger speaks so darkly about; and as Professor Morison points out:

> Violence has probably been less common in American society than in many other nations, such as Mexico; and our waves of violence, excepting those derived from a fast-moving frontier to which no rule of law had been extended, can be paralleled by those in other coun-

tries. . . . how about the bloody scenes of successive French, Russian, and Mexican revolutions?[172]

Little wonder that today's younger Americans, having been presented a wholly distorted view of the American past, have contempt for our traditions. When those traditions are attacked, they have almost no way of knowing the great achievements and strengths that far overshadow the evils—which no nation in history has been without.

[172]"Violence and History," Letters to the Editor, *Saturday Review* (June 15, 1968).

XIX

The True American Tradition and the Triple Revolutions

Historians will differ on whether the political philosophy and the military economic direction of any nation has changed more fundamentally than those of the United States in a comparable period of time—1933-1967.

But as an eye witness to governmental and other public action throughout these years, I have formed the opinion that the United States merits the distinction of having discarded its past and meaning in one of the briefest spans of modern history.[173] [Former New York *Times* correspondent and author Arthur Krock.]

Can a nation, having discarded its past and its meaning, escape the consequences of such an act? The violence, lawlessness, and social disruption that has engulfed the nation in recent years suggest it cannot. When a country cuts itself off from its historical experience and the principles that allowed it to flourish, it is like a giant ocean liner on a dark fogbound sea without a philosophical rudder or radar to guide it. And almost no one today denies that somehow, two hundred years after signing the Declaration of Independence, we have lost our sense of direction and our bold daring as a nation.

This loss of direction can be traced to the fact that the American Revolution of 1776 is an "interrupted revolution." It still remains for Americans to complete the moral, philosophical, and political goals of the Founders, to finish what they began almost two hundred years ago.

We began, as most of us know, with a profound sense of direction, provided by perhaps the most remarkable group of men ever to come together in one period of history. It is quite correct to point out, as many historians do to an excessive degree, that the Founders defaulted in not abolishing slavery. It was one of a number of moral compromises which was to cost the country dearly in the decades after the American Revolution of 1776. Such a default illustrates what

---

[173] *Memoirs—Sixty Years on the Firing Line*, excerpts reprinted in the *Congressional Record* (September 23, 1968).

a powerful influence, for good or ill, the dead can have on the living.

But what would the Founders say about those individuals and groups who initiate violence and about those who went to the August 1968 Democratic Convention to foment disruption in an effort to influence political decisions? What would they say of these same groups who have, throughout most of the 1960s, justified the use of violence as in the tradition of the American Revolution of 1776?

The Failure and Success of Two Revolutions

First, the Founders might compare today's New Left radicals not with themselves, but with the radicals of the late eighteenth century who precipitated the French Revolution. The Founders, while in sympathy with the aims of the French Revolution, at the onset might point out that its failure was rooted in its lack of understanding of what was to come after the revolution. Like today's New Left, the French Revolutionaries knew how to tear down, but had only a vague notion what they wanted in the wake of the ouster of the French monarchy.

The minds who created and carried forth the American Revolution knew what they wanted, although they went through a period of groping for the form their post-revolution government would take. Most important, the Founders drew heavily on the philosophy of reason, rights, and individual liberty as enunciated by John Locke. The French Revolutionaries had largely rejected Locke in favor of the collectivist and egalitarian philosophy of Jean Jacques Rousseau, who died almost twenty years before the French Revolution. In tribute to Rousseau as the philosophical precursor of the revolution, his remains were removed from Ermenonville, France, to the Pantheon in Paris during the revolution. Contemporary historical analyses of Karl Marx rarely reveal that the father of modern Socialism drew great inspiration from Rousseau and from Rousseau's beliefs that men were victims of their environment and of the exploitation of an active and wealthy few. Rousseau also believed that the size and complexity of eighteenth century France and Europe created inequality and injustice; what was needed to correct such abuses was the creation of a small and simple egalitarian state. Today the New Left expresses many of the same ideas, in such terms as "decentralization" and in calls for small collective communes or communities where everyone shares his good (or bad) fortune with his fellow man.

These two fundamentally different philosophical views determined the direction, course, and character of the American and French Revolutions. The effects of the contrasting philosophies—the Founders' emphasis on individualism and the French Revolutionists' emphasis on collectivism—also were evident in the decade after both eighteenth century revolutions.

France quickly fell victim to a series of dictatorships in the nineteenth century. There are many scholars who believe France's endless trouble through the nineteenth and twentieth centuries can ultimately be traced back to the failure of the French Revolution.

In contrast, the American Revolution of 1776 constructed a system that was responsible for the most remarkable social, political, and economic revolution in the history of mankind. This was the legacy left to the future generations of Americans by a small band of brilliant men, just as a very small group left a legacy of a negative nature to the French people after the revolution of 1789. While the French Declaration of Rights of August 17, 1789, was based on the American Declaration of Independence, its failure to produce the same results as our own declaration was due to the difference in the philosophy held by the Founders and that held by those who gave expression and leadership to the French Revolution. In reality, only one revolution of the last two hundred years has succeeded in its original goals, while all others have degenerated into a more cruel form of suppression than that which each revolution sought to supplant; that one is the American Revolution of 1776.

Ours was a revolution that drew on an affirmative philosophy that had been emerging in western society for centuries —the philosophy of freedom and individualism under which every man was to be responsible for his own survival.

Today, those New Left radicals who went to Chicago and continue to disrupt college campuses hold a basic philosophy of collectivism. In political terms, they wish to see a program of state socialism enacted, supplanting the private economic and political system that has its roots in the American Revolution of 1776.

If the Founders could comment on the New Left today, they undoubtedly would state that, should the New Left succeed in the decades ahead, they will end up destroying the very political, social, and economic freedom that the 1776 Revolution made possible.

The True Tradition

Americans, old as well as young, need to rediscover the principles upon which America was founded. They also need to understand the profound philosophical influences the American Revolution had on nineteenth and twentieth century America. Those influences, combined with two other events in the decade of the 1770s, were to shape the most profound political, social, and material revolution in mankind's history.

First, the Declaration of Independence and the U.S. Constitution were the concrete expression of the intellectual and philosophical thoughts and goals of their framers. Second, in the same year the Declaration of Independence was signed, Adam Smith published the first, and for almost a hundred years thereafter, the finest treatise on free economic thought, *The Wealth of Nations*.

Liberals in all their ignorance and Socialists and Marxists in all their guile regard Smith's *The Wealth of Nations* as "the fundamentalist bible of the old dog-eat-dog type of businessmen." This is the way the distinguished author of *The Roots of Capitalism*, John Chamberlain, claims his professors in the 1920s regarded Smith's monumental work. But this same treatise profoundly influenced the framers of the U.S. Constitution of 1789. Thomas Jefferson, for example, praised *The Wealth of Nations* for its "sheer genius," and acknowledged its influence on him in authoring the Declaration of Independence.

With considerable candor, Mr. Chamberlain acknowledges that as a student he never read *The Wealth of Nations*, although he now wishes he had. He contends that it "should be restored to its cornerstone position in any institution that pretends to teach the subject of economics."

Smith was writing for the ages out of a study that encompassed the whole millennial experience of European man . . . drawing upon everything European man had been doing since he came out of the Dark Ages, and even before, to fashion a science of economics that would be good for all time.[174]

Just as Sir Isaac Newton studied and pondered the laws of

---

[174] *The Wealth of Nations*, Introduction, (New York; Arlington House).

nature through observations, so Smith studied the laws of human action and arrived at certain universal principles which would apply to all men in all ages. To the same degree in the political world, the Founders of the American system studied past forms of government and profited by the lessons offered by the history of European man prior to 1776.

The Wealth of Nations formed the theoretical economic foundation for the Industrial Revolution in concord with the Declaration of Independence and the U.S. Constitution.

The social and political system inherent in the Declaration of Independence and the U.S. Consitution provided the freedom for every man to be the founder of his own fortune. And this system created the geographical unity for trade and cooperation among the states of the union. Such freedom and unity developed the climate necessary for the unprecedented burst of creative energies that culminated in the countless mechanical inventions and industries of nineteenth century America, and became the foundation for today's technological revolution and its resulting material abundance and affluence. Thus our material wealth today is the direct result of the events of the nineteenth century which were made possible by the freedom won in the Revolution of 1776.

Events, good or bad, are not causeless. They are the direct result of men's thinking and planning, or lack of it, and of the philosophy they hold: which means of their way of looking at the world.

In a profound, affirmative way, the Founders studied the past and all the lessons it offered, and constructed an original, uniquely American, free social and political system. The Founders also looked deeply into the nature of human beings, seeking by their efforts to harmonize their thinking with the natural state of men and women. The Founders came to the conclusion that the natural state of man was to be free and that he had within him the potential to act responsibly if offered a set of principles and a philosophy. What is staggering about this achievement is that such a benevolent outlook toward men had never before been professed, let alone expressed in a workable, concrete social system.

The American and Industrial Revolutions were the product of less than one hundred *free minds*: the Founders of America and men like Adam Smith. It was in the same year the Declaration of Independence was signed that Adam Smith first published his work on free economics, *The Wealth of*

Nations. And, in the same decade, the 1770s, another momentous event occurred: the invention of the steam engine by Watt.

James Watt and John Wilkinson, a pioneer ironmaster and inventor of precision cutting tools, joined forces in the Boulton Watt Company to produce the first workable and saleable steam engine—the forerunner of the steam locomotive and railway equipment which would unite nations and continents.

Thus, in one decade, the Founders laid the political and social foundation for the Industrial Revolution of the nineteenth century. Smith's *The Wealth of Nations* laid the theoretical economic foundation, that is, the practical principles to guide men of productive genius. James Watt's invention of the steam engine laid the physical foundation.

The Industrial Revolution unleashed energies and inventive capacities that poured forth a profusion of material achievements that defied all the Marxist and Socialist sour predictions that the Industrial Age would impoverish the masses. As a matter of fact, it is most probable that without our political system, America would have degenerated into a kind of industrial feudalism that characterized nineteenth century Germany or the Nazi and Communist industrial totalitarian states of the twentieth century—assuming industrial advances would even have been possible without the American political system, for they have not been matched in any other nation under any other political form.

Unlike other nations of the last two centuries which exacted from their peoples a staggering and often hideous price for economic and social progress, the Industrial Revolution in America came about without the use of force or compulsion or great human sacrifice; men were free to be the founders of their own fortunes, as the Founding Fathers had envisioned. The standard of living of the masses was raised to heights not even yet obtained in collective societies, human life was lengthened and strengthened, and the stage was set for the Technological Revolution of this century. From the Industrial Revolution came all the basic inventions and industries and scientific knowledge upon which the Capitalists and their intellectual partners—scientists, inventors, and engineers—would improve in the short six decades of our twentieth century.

The Interrupted Revolution
Almost two hundred years after the signing of the Declara-

tion of Independence we have yet to make a consistent way of life of the philosophy and principles the Founders gave this nation. After 150 years of living close to their philosophy we detoured from the historic highroad they set us upon. The American Revolution of 1776 is an interrupted and incomplete revolution; the violent conflicts and disorders of the 1960s are a consequence of this little-appreciated historical fact.

The interruption of the American Revolution was not a sudden development; a gradual undermining of the philosophy and principles of 1776 began in earnest after the U.S. Civil War. Even before the Civil War, the seeds of ideas that had not yet even sprouted roots created fears in the minds of a few thinkers. The lucid warnings they put forth, about the possible fate of the American Republic if we did not preserve and protect the principles of the Founders, are startling in the context of the 1968 Chicago uprising and the regularity of America's current widespread violence. In a letter to an American friend dated May 23, 1857, Thomas Macauley looked into the future and warned:

> Either some Caesar or Napoleon will seize the reins of government with a strong hand; or your Republic [the United States] will be as fearfully plundered and laid waste by the barbarians in the twentieth century as the Roman Empire was in the fifth—with this difference . . . that your Huns and vandals will have been engendered *within your own country by your own institutions*. [My emphasis.]

Just how prophetic was Macaulay? Merely consider the counterrevolution of ideas that took shape after 1865; the formulation of these ideas in political action beginning in 1933; and the violent manifestation of these ideas in street warfare, waged by counterrevolutionaries who call themselves the New Left.

XX
The Counterrevolution—The Wrecking of a Republic

When a civilization declines it is through no mystic limitation of corporate life, but through the failure of its political and intellectual leadership to meet the challenge of change.[175]

In an affirmative sense, we can see the truth of Will and Ariel Durant's statement above by an opposite, the Founding Fathers. As intellectual and political leaders, they formulated a series of ideas which transformed a wilderness into a world power in a dramatically short period of time. From the latter nineteenth century through most of the twentieth the dominant political and intellectual leaders have formulated ideas in complete contrast to those of the Founders. Now, in the second half of this century, those political ideas are being questioned and acknowledged as the cause for social chaos and unrest.

It does not serve the cause of freedom, social concord, and human progress to shift the burden of blame and assign collective guilt to American society or, as a Presidential Commission on Civil Disorders did in 1968, to cite the cause of urban riots as the product of "white racism." To evade the central and all-important role that political and intellectual leadership plays in the life and death of a nation is to concede that the role of leaders is unimportant and has no influence on a nation. But, in fact, such leadership formulates the ideas and offers inspiration that forms a nation's character and upon which its citizens act, for better or worse.

America has come to its current chaos because the intellectual, moral, and political leadership have acted on a set of ideas that arose in the nineteenth century. In the midst of the unprecedented achievements of the nineteenth century Industrial Revolution, a group of intellectuals in America felt left out and unrewarded by the newly emerging industrial

---

[175] Will and Ariel Durant, *The Lessons of History* (New York; Simon & Schuster, 1968), condensed in *Reader's Digest* (December, 1968), p. 273.

era. Unable or unwilling to understand the true and positive nature of the new emerging industrial era as a product of freedom, many such intellectuals were intent on controlling or subverting with the power of government the Industrial Revolution. Holding a philosophy that stood for collectivism and state control of the lives of the people and the means of economic production, such men and women stood as a counterrevolutionary force to the principles of the Founders based on individualism and the limited power of the state. In the latter nineteenth century, such intellectuals—many Marxists and Socialists—sought to smear and distort the achievements of the Founding Fathers and of the industrial and inventive geniuses of the nineteenth century. One American Marxist historian, Charles Beard, even insisted that the motivation of the Founders for framing the U.S. Constitution was materialistic, geared toward their own economic profit. Other less prominent Socialist intellectuals imputed evil motives to the nineteenth century industrialists who, ironically, helped by their wealth to build universities. From these very centers of learning, such intellectuals began a wholesale attack on the foundations of the American and Industrial Revolutions—an attack which many who made the industrial era did not understand or know how to answer. This attack went largely unchallenged during the latter nineteenth century and remains so to this very day. Eventually the attempt to interrupt and subvert the achievements of the revolutions of the eighteenth and nineteenth centuries in America climaxed in the election of the FDR New Deal in 1933. Just as the influences the Founders set into motion in 1776 did not find their greatest fulfillment until decades later, so the efforts of America's counterrevolutionaries, begun in the nineteenth century, did not come into concrete political form until 1933.

Roosevelt's Counterrevolution

The New Deal was said to have been a necessary response to the Great Depression—allegedly caused by the collapse of the free economic system for which the Founders and Adam Smith had helped lay the foundation. And for years many Americans have blamed former President Hoover for the economic calamity of the 1930s. But the real cause for the Great Depression was neither the weakness nor abuses in the private enterprise sector nor the mistakes of one man. The real cause was the growing government intervention in the still young, free economic market. It is forgotten that this country, in terms of decades, is still relatively new—roughly only three hundred years old.

The Great Depression of the 1930s was the direct result of attempts to control freedom by government—causing factors directly opposed to the principles of free enterprise, and of the Founding Fathers who insisted on limiting the function of government. Between the end of the U.S. Civil War and the election of FDR, intellectuals who sought to subvert the principles and achievements of the American and Industrial Revolutions influenced certain political leaders allegedly to correct abuses and "monopolies" caused by big business and the private economic system. But these monopolies arose *because* city, state, and Federal governments used their power to close out competition by politically influential businessmen; and each government-imposed "correction" of abuses undercut the natural working of free economics, making the situation much worse until, by the 1920s, the private economic sector collapsed in a momentary crisis. Abroad, as in America, the worldwide depression after World War I could be traced directly to the unwise and unworkable attempts of government to "plan" and "control" the working of free markets and free men. In seeking to direct the economic destiny of its citizens, such nations as the United States brought about the very calamity they meant to ensure against.

Instead of removing these life-bleeding controls and restraints on freedom, the Roosevelt New Deal added still more government controls. When spending schemes did not cure the Great Depression, but only drugged it, Roosevelt turned to the oldest solution known to men and nations: he began gearing American industry for war. In doing so he committed a former free economy, which profits in the long run more from peace than war, to a warfare and welfare state economy. After World War II this debt-ridden, regulation-smothered system grew into a "cold war" economy, committed to huge government contracts for national defense and space efforts. The prosperity we enjoy today is due largely to that sector of the economy that is relatively free, to a deficit system of economics, and to the huge outlays by government which depend on the still-healthy sector for support. There is a direct relationship between rising outlays for social welfare handouts and the rising rate of taxation, corporate as well as private. With growth of government has come controls. The vio-

lence and chaos of today is the direct result of those government controls and their inability to work.

Government force is failing, where freedom can succeed.
Today, the largest segment of the nation is the government—
which has now established itself to lead, by force if necessary, a national economy and its people toward the future
clouded by chaos, violence, and unrest. In no small measure,
the distortion of our economic and political life that began
under FDR made possible the violence and upheavals of the
1960s. The machinery of government, built over the decades
since the 1930s, is breaking down under its own deficiencies
and size. Professor Peter Drucker of New York University has
observed:

> Modern government has become ungovernable. There
> is no government today that can claim control of its
> bureaucracy and of its various agencies. . . . This is a
> threat to the basic capacity of government to give direc-
> tion and leadership.[176]

In the cities of our nation this breakdown has made possible the rise of radical political elements who seize upon the
inability of government to provide promised social services to
assault violently the entire social and political system. Therefore, criticism that government is a danger, heard in the past
only from more conservative circles, now transcends ideological and political party lines.

The fuller meaning of the collapse of Liberalism, dominant
since the 1930s, can be grasped by briefly reviewing the record of Liberalism at home and abroad:

> **Urban Centers**—Today's Liberals lament that Ameri-
> can cities are in a state of collapse and decay—urban
> centers over which Liberalism has had political control
> for many decades. However, the prescription offered to
> cure our cities is bottomed on the same philosophy
> which brought about the crisis in the first place: more
> state and federal aid (taxes), and control.
>
> **Civil Disorders**—Liberalism gave active encouragement
> to the civil rights and student protest groups in the early
> part of the 1960s, which sought forced equality through
> protest marches. Having now unleashed powerful and
> destructive forces in the streets, Liberals are bewildered
> and unable to cope with the barbarism that has engulfed
> the nation.

---

[176] The New York *Times* (March 4, 1969).

Welfare—Liberals gave birth to widespread public welfare handouts. Today, few deny the evils produced by this approach. To cure the problem, however, the Liberal solution, like the New Left solution, is a more radical form of the same system: guaranteed annual incomes. Yet the current welfare system has already exhausted city and state budgets; so Liberals now call for the Federal government to assume the burden.

Fiscal Taxes—While government leaders long vowed that social programs were for the people, swollen city, state, and federal budgets have not only robbed the productive and the nonproductive alike, but have placed the earnings of those very masses in serious jeopardy with rampaging inflation. The growth of repressive taxation since the end of World War II has produced not "soak the rich" as was its original motivation but "soak the prosperous and poor alike."

Education—No part of the Liberal program has been given greater attention or passion than education. Today, however, there is almost no one on the high school or college level, liberal or conservative, black or white, who does not confess that American education is beset by a serious crisis. Instead of examining the philosophy upon which education rests, the supporters of modern education persist in the delusion that what is needed to arrest the crisis is more funds and moral fervor. They ignore the crucial need for intellectual ideas, for teaching the connection between ideas and events—that philosophy precedes action (and politics). In no small measure, the revolt in our universities can be traced directly to the lack of these teachings, and to the inadequacies of Liberal education. A minority of revolutionaries have seized on the fact of decay in educational institutions and are using it for the larger purpose of attacking, maiming, and eventually destroying the social system that supports these educational institutions.

Foreign Policy—Since the onset of the New Deal, America has fought one major war and two "police actions." Thousands have died, and enormous wealth has been expended; yet Korea's armistice was inconclusive, and in Vietnam we are fighting a foe who declares its aim to be victory while we vacillate despite definite military advantages. After World War II, Liberal blindness, delusion, and compromise led to the triumph of totalitarian Communism in Czechoslavakia, Yugoslavia, Hungary, and other Eastern European countries, and in China and North Vietnam in Asia. Liberal delusion, too, during

the Eisenhower and Kennedy Administrations led to
Communism's triumph near our own shores: Cuba.

Foreign Aid—New Deal Liberalism squandered bil-
lions on an international scale with results that have
been no less disastrous than at home. The Liberals' re-
ward for their role as social worker either abroad or at
home has been unprecedented hatred and enmity from
friends as well as foes.

Perhaps a more ominous legacy of Liberalism is noted in
the comment of author John Dos Passos who observed that
the Populist Louisiana Governor of the 1930s, Huey Long,
had once remarked "If Fascism comes to America it will
come as Anti-Fascism." Dos Passos then observed:

> Twenty-three years after Franklin Roosevelt's death,
> we face the dislocations to which the elephantiasis of the
> New Deal's bureaucratic organizations have largely contri-
> buted. Furthermore, we suffer from the essential shoddi-
> ness of much of the philosophy which underlay New Deal
> thinking. In the organized disorder ravaging American
> cities and disrupting the colleges we begin to recognize
> what Huey Long meant by American Fascism.[177]

Mr. Tugwell Tells the Truth

If we are to deal intelligently with the crisis and anarchy in
America today, we must recognize that the attempt to man-
age our swollen and oversized government as it is, offers little
prospect of genuine success. The reason for this lies in the
profound contradiction on which America has tried to operate since the 1933 New Deal.

Since FDR's counterrevolution against the principles of
1776 and 1789, our nation has tried to straddle the principles
of both Revolutions: the 1776 Revolution's principles of protection of rights and limited government, and the 1933 revolution's principles of growing government that often lead to
violation of individual rights. Neither an individual nor a nation can serve two masters. Abraham Lincoln stated this principle in a different context in his "House Divided" speech of
June 16, 1858:

> A house divided against itself cannot stand. I do not
> expect the house to fall but I do expect it will cease to
> be divided. It will become all one thing or all another.

---

[177] John Dos Passos, *op. cit.*)

So it is in a nation divided between the force of government on one hand and individual freedom on the other; it will become all one thing, or all the other. The violence, anarchy, and social discord of the 1960s exemplify the inability of the American republic to remain divided. The New Left radicals and revolutionaries would unite the nation under the banner of statism. To do this they would need to abandon the Revolution of 1776, and carry the counterrevolution of 1933 to its ultimate end: the totalitarian state.

Defenders of the New Deal will claim that it was a necessary and not a counterrevolutionary movement. They will cite the "promote the general welfare" clause in the Constitution as a justification for the legislation from the New Deal to the present, as proof that such legislation was or is in concert with the spirit and letter of the U.S. Constitution.

But one of the architects of the New Deal, Rexford Tugwell, now a member of the Center for the Study of Democratic Institutions, tells us rather candidly that the social legislation passed by the New Deal and successive administrations would have been greatly frowned on by the Founders and was often in complete contradiction to the U.S. Constitution. Tugwell tells us that such arguments as the citing of the "promote the general welfare" clause

> . . . were tortured interpretations of a document intended to prevent them. The Government did expect responsibility for individual well being and did interfere to make it secure. But it really had to be admitted that it was done irregularly and *according to the doctrine that the framers would have rejected*. Despite constantly reiterated declarations that what was being done was in pursuit of aims embodied in the Constitution of 1789, obviously it was in contravention to them. . . ."[178] [My emphasis.]

Both James Madison and Thomas Jefferson were very specific as to the phrase "promote the general welfare," Madison warning during debate in the First Congress over subsidy to Cape Cod fishermen that such an interpretation

> . . . would subvert the very foundations, and transmute the very nature of the limited government established by the people of America.[179]

---

[178] Rexford Tugwell, The New York *Times* (March 10, 1968).
[179] James Madison, *The Federalist Papers*, No. 83.

When the bill was defeated, Jefferson expressed the hope that the issue of the "promote the general welfare" clause would

> . . . settle forever the meaning of this phrase, which by mere grammatical quibble, has countenanced the general Government in a claim of universal power.[180]

Do We Need a New Constitution?

Rexford Tugwell made this startling admission as part of his argument for the adoption of a new constitution, a document that would guarantee social, not individual, rights. Some of these "social" rights would be a guaranteed income, education, housing, and medical care provided by government.

The Founders of America believed that the foundation of a free society rests on political liberty, individual rights, and the protection by government of such rights, not on economic security. The Founders understood in the most profound sense that political and individual rights gave to each citizen of a country control of his own life, to make of that life whatever he wanted, to go as far in a career as his talents would take him, to make as much money as he could, to choose his own way of life so long as it did not violate the rights of others. The Founders were convinced that men and women with freedom, political and individual rights would not only act responsibly and within reason, but that such ideas would pave the way for economic progress if the force of freedom were allowed to work.

It was, however, the illusion of certain economic security, among many factors, which led the German people in the 1920s and 1930s to embrace the program of Adolph Hitler's National Socialism; their tragic choice came after years, before and after World War I, under a welfare state similar to what has developed in America since the FDR New Deal of 1933. Another factor in bringing Hitler to power and moving Germany beyond its welfare state to full State Socialism was the use of violence for political ends—not unlike that which we have seen in our universities and cities, and very much like that at the Democratic Convention in Chicago in August

---

[180]Thomas Jefferson, letter to Albert Gallatin, 1817, published in *The Political Writings of Thomas Jefferson* (New York; The Liberal Arts Press, 1955).

1968. Street violence in Germany began developing in the 1920s when the welfare state was buckling under the demands and pressures generated by German intellectual, political, and moral leadership.

Is a similar situation developing in the United States? The Center for the Study of Democratic Institutions seeks a "new constitution" for America. This West Coast-based organization, considered by many to be far to the radical left politically, helped create The National Conference for New Politics. The NCNP was formed at the Center in 1965; at the Democratic Convention in August 1968, many of its members, inside and outside the Chicago Convention, engaged in violence allegedly in an effort to prevent the nomination of then Vice President Hubert Humphrey. Political observers have pointed out, however, that the violence was actually an attempt by more radical elements to take over and control the Democratic Party in 1972—the year it is supposed Massachusetts Senator Edward M. Kennedy will make his bid for the Presidential nomination. Edward Kennedy, brother of the late John and Robert Kennedy, has been more and more identified with positions of the Center for the Study of Democratic Institutions and its goals, such as a "new constitution." The Senator himself has not publicly advocated such a radical move, but a close friend and associate of his, former aide and confidante to John and Robert Kennedy, Theodore Sorenson, has said in print he supports such a concept. Sorenson is believed eager to seek in 1970 the New York U.S. Senate seat held by the assassinated Robert Kennedy.

In fact, the rise of the radical New Left in America under the banner of the "New Politics" is a political movement intent on taking the nation beyond Franklin Roosevelt's philosophy of more government in the political, social, and economic areas of American life. Such political radicals would take us farther away from the principles and philosophy of the Founders. In allowing a piecemeal discarding of our past and its meaning as the moral cement for the American civilization, we have without question shaped the conditions that created the violence and anarchy that have engulfed the nation in general and the 1968 Democratic Convention in particular. Such events are the physical manifestation of the collapse of a philosophy that believed, from its start in the last century, that it could abandon reason and freedom in favor of force.

Since the end of the American Civil War, we have seen a counterrevolutionary—as well as reactionary—intellectual movement gut the genius of a remarkable political and social system in a piecemeal fashion. So swift a virtual wrecking of a republican form of government stands as one of the great tragedies of the twentieth century. Unwilling to learn the lessons of European history, the intellectuals opposed to the philosophy of the Founders in the last century have left a great civilization that is America disarmed and bewildered. The legacy American Liberals have left the American people —despite their well meaning but misguided motivation—is one of violence, chaos, and the crucial danger that at some future date we could, as a people, be cast beyond the twilight that is today's violence into a new Dark Age.

Such a state of affairs was brought about by philosophical currents of thought, articulated by intellectual, political, and moral leaders who would reverse the human progress so painfully achieved over the centuries. Only by an affirmative philosophy, such as that expressed by the Founders, articulated by men of reason, will human liberty and progress recover its lost ground.

XXI

Finishing the Work of the Founders – An Age of Reform and Repeal

The men who founded your republic had an uncommonly clear grasp of the general ideas that they wanted ... I know of only three times in the western world when statesmen consciously took control of historic destinies: Periclean Athens, Rome under Augustus, and the founding of your American republic.[181] *[British Philosopher Alfred North Whitehead.]*

The establishment of the American Republic defied not only Mother England, but when the Federal Constitution of 1789 was ratified, it defied the prediction of every previous political scientist who thought such a system of government impossible. And still it stands, as Harvard historian Samuel Eliot Morison has stated, as, "the most original contribution of the United States to the history and technique of human liberty."[182]

What we witness in the violence and social discord of the last decade is the tragic consequence of a century of growing revolt from our past and its meaning, and the discarding of an affirmative philosophical gyroscope for a great nation.

The crucial question remaining is whether we can fashion a freedom manifesto that embodies the essential philosophy, principles, and political program of the framers of the U.S. Constitution. We need to finish what the Founders began, translating such a paramount effort into a practical political program that embodies the concept of an "Age of Reform and Repeal": reform in those areas that conflict with the Constitution, and repeal of those measures which violate both the Declaration of Independence and the U.S. Constitution as well as their underlying concepts of individual liberty and the philosophy of reason.

---

[181]Lucien Price, Ed. *The Diologues of Alfred North Whitehead* (Atlantic-Little Brown & Co., 1954), p. 203.

[182]*The Oxford History of The American People* (New York; Oxford University Press, 1965), p. 316.

Americans who recoil in righteous anger at force, violence, and the flight from freedom such actions portend, must not sit back and either lament such actions or give only lip service to documents like the U.S. Declaration of Independence. As great as they are, this and the U.S. Constitution are only as strong as the honesty and integrity of the men and women who use them, interpret them, and defend them. When a nation's citizens loose sight of its meaning, a document loses all its moral or actual power, and force fills the place where once freedom—the archenemy of violence, evil, and disruption—stood supreme.

America needs a freedom manifesto in these troubled times; and a new and dynamic leadership that will help thoughtful and concerned Americans rediscover the ideals, philosophy, and political program of the Founding Fathers. This does not mean "going back," for the philosophy of the Founders is one for all ages; born of harsh struggle, intellectual conflict, tested by time in the laboratory which is life experience.

If millions of Americans feel that their lives are bereft of meaning because of what the current intellectual, political, and moral leadership has offered them in the way of policies of force and compulsion, they need not feel that no alternative exists. Alternatives *do* exist. We must take the time and patience to rediscover those principles of reason, individualism, protection of rights, liberty, and law by due process.

The Founders of the American Republic, in their dedication to these verities, helped produce the most successful and remarkable social system in the history of mankind. Those whom the whole world was watching in Chicago in August 1968 were acting on principles and a philosophy that would create a system of elitist rule, which would suffocate and strangle that very freedom which Western man has struggled so long and hard to achieve. Freedom lost the day to brute force in Chicago, as it has been losing ground in all of this century, more swiftly since the counterrevolutionary movement in 1933. If men of reason remain mere spectators to what went on in Chicago it could well be that in some future time, we will no longer be allowed the luxury and liberty of being spectators, but will be the very oppressed subjects of those whom the whole world was watching during that August week.

The divisions which have beset the nation in the 1960s are an accurate, ugly confirmation of the struggle between two philosophies which has for decades been confined to the political world. It is not surprising that the Chicago Convention should bring into violent, open conflict the philosophical principles of the Revolution of 1776 and the counterrevolution of 1933.

The events in Chicago, and those before on our nation's college campuses and in our cities, have finally taken this struggle from the political stage into the arena of physical force and disruption. The authors of such anarchy, however, are the very Liberal intellectuals who assumed for years that they could straddle the principles of both revolutions: one founded on freedom, and one founded on the counter philosophy of force.

The violence of Chicago and in the nation in general is frighteningly similar to what happened in an earlier period of Western history. For the very philosophy that led to Nazism, Communism, and Fascism in Europe served the same basic philosophical premises held by those who went to Chicago to commit violence and disruption. If we take such premises to their logical ends, we cannot help but draw the conclusion that what we shall ultimately produce is not peace, prosperity, and order, but a technological totalitarianism, such as that George Orwell understood could come if certain changes were not made in the drift and decay of Western society.

Reform, Repeal, Power Dispersal

Perhaps no more serious problem faces the nation in the second half of this century than the current crisis of intellectual, political, and moral leadership. Any continued Liberal stewardship of our domestic and foreign affairs is more than likely to compound those very problems that Liberalism made possible.

What is needed in America is reorganization of our political life. This is not the "me-too" Republican reaction to Liberalism, nor the often inadequate Conservative approach, nor the essentially "mini-welfare state" approach of the Populist George Wallace who masqueraded as an alternative to LBJ's Great Society. An intelligent political program is required for that large and essentially unrepresented majority of Americans who find the current approaches inadequate. What is mandatory is not some national political third party, but an independent intellectual force which takes as its task the political goals of reform, repeal, and power dispersal.

What this movement should do is construct a program that

seeks reform in those areas which are in contradiction to the principles, philosophy, and goals of the Founders of America. This would mean, in tangible terms, "reform" from top to bottom of the tax structure, a lifting of the arbitrary and artificial restraints on business, and of compulsive features that place individual laborers in the position of being forced to join unions. It would also mean the drastic curbing, if not dissolution, of federal regulatory agencies.

As to "repeal," we should repeal those laws which not only conflict with the principles of the Founders, but which interfere with the life, liberty, and pursuit of happiness of the individual. This would mean, as one crucial example, the abolition of the military draft and its replacement by a volunteer army. It would mean, too, the repeal of those laws which give agencies like the Federal Communications Commission almost unlimited power to act as a quasi-censor of the broadcasting industry in direct violation of the First Amendment.

In matters of "power dispersal," such a program would entail breaking up concentrations of political, economic, and government power and dispersing it to the states. In economic terms it would mean removing the legal monopoly held by industries such as telephone, gas, oil, shipping, and airlines which enjoy either direct subsidy or monopoly by legislation; and throwing these industries open to the free market economy. In matters of indirect subsidy, those churches or religious groups which engage in any business enterprise (real estate, broadcasting, stock portfolios) should pay their share of income, corporation, and personal income taxes—as does the Mormon Church which voluntarily pays income taxes on business ventures. The current indirect subsidy of the religious faiths of America contravenes the Founders' well-grounded belief in the separation of the Church and the State.

1976: Reference Point for Reform

In 1976 we will observe the 200th anniversary of the signing of the Declaration of Independence. What we should celebrate during the Bicentennial is the achievement of a handful of brilliant men who gave a nation a dynamic beginning and a sense of direction. It was, as pointed out earlier, the foundation for one of the most remarkable social, political, and economic revolutions in the history of mankind. These two hundred years could correctly be called "The Era of the Triple

Revolution": the American, the Industrial, and the Technological.

The Bicentennial celebration can serve as a rallying point for the proposed "Age of Reform, Repeal, and Power Dispersal." However, it is clear that some political and intellectual leaders mean to use the Bicentennial for political purposes that are in contradiction to the philosophy of the Founders.

The Boston Bicentennial Commission has not taken as its theme individualism, reason, and protection of rights, as the Founders set forth. Rather, Boston is stressing the Liberal and left-wing premise of "interdependence" and its subsidiary theme of "building a better urban America." This plan completely ignores the affirmative aspects—and the very existence—of the American Revolution and of the subsequent Industrial and Technological Revolutions.

One member of Philadelphia's Bicentennial Commission is former Democratic Senator Joseph Clark, whose philosophy of government is hardly representative of those whom Philadelphia is reputedly commemorating. In fact, the philosophy which former Senator Clark espouses is very much in tune with the counterrevolutionary movement that began under FDR and the New Deal.

These illustrations serve to point out how America's political, intellectual, and moral leadership (including business leaders) have come to accept the premises of the counterrevolutionaries. They are giving lip service to the United States Constitution and the Declaration of Independence by celebrating in the name of freedom; but it is in name alone, for they are not forming their celebrations on the principles of these two profound documents nor of the men who structured them.

During his 1968 political campaign, Richard M. Nixon pledged "new leadership." He also expressed a desire to bind up and heal the divisions that beset our nation. However, we can deal with today's divisions and conflicts between various social, political, and economic groups only if we understand the underlying philosophy which brought them about—for philosophy must precede action.

President Nixon has sought to correct the clear, if not lethal, contradiction between the philosophy of individual freedom and that of the current compulsive draft laws. Perhaps more than any previous President, Mr. Nixon is in a position to help lead or at least give his support to the political program of "Reform, Repeal, and Power Dispersal." In shaping and planning the Federal Government's own plans for the 1976 celebration, Mr. Nixon can help emphasize the true American tradition and aim his program toward the moral majority of the younger generation, charging them with the goal of finishing the work of the Founders. As the occupant of an office that has potentially enormous moral leadership, he would be offering to America's young the leadership and sense of direction they are searching for.

The Real Revolutionists

Those who were in the streets of Chicago in August 1968 and who continue to initiate violence and disruption in our cities and on our college campuses are not real revolutionaries. They are intellectual thugs and hoodlums. The Founders of America were the only real revolutionaries of the last two hundred years, largely because they sought to effect their own revolution based on reason and natural law. Theirs was a revolution that sought to affirm life; those in Chicago sought to negate life, liberty, and human achievement and progress.

What America, if not the entire Western civilization, needs is a group of broad-gauged intellectual and political leaders who speak and act in the true tradition of the American revolution, a revolution that has been interrupted while still incomplete. We have yet to fulfill the highest aspirations the Founders had for this nation and its people; hopes born, not of fuzzy-wishful-thinking men, but of men dedicated to the philosophy of individualism, reason, free economic enterprise, and liberty under law and due process. Theirs was a hope and a set of principles to which men of all ages and all nations can proudly repair.

The task of summoning a society to finish the work of its founders is not to be accomplished by slogans and clichés; but by a firm and consistent intelligent understanding of the philosophical base to which we must proudly and confidently turn in answering the violent assaults of America's enemies, without as well as within, and especially in answering the questioning of our youth.

History tells us many things. One is that no nation ever dies without a clear cause. The rise and fall of great nations is the direct result of good and bad ideas: a judgment we make by looking realistically at how both good and bad ideas affect a nation or a civilization. Today, almost two hundred years after our birth, we have an opportunity to make a comparison between two different and diametrically opposed ideas of how men shall govern themselves: the first 150 years under the concept of the Founders, and most of this century under the concept of the power of the state. The tragedies that have befallen nations in Europe in this century are both a warning and a lesson, for the United States is traveling the same road, and has been since the 1933 counterrevolution.

All other so-called revolutionaries sought power over people. Understanding the evils that even well-meaning men in power could inflict on their fellow countrymen, the Founders sought not power over people, but the unleashing of the power within individual people. It was a moral compact they drew up among themselves; an affirmation of life, liberty, and of the conviction that men could be the captains of their own destinies if given proper moral and philosophical principles.

In the second half of this century, America is faced with a crucial choice between three alternatives. 1. We can submit to the forces of the New Left who have made it clear that their solution to our mounting problems is not less government, but more government—to go beyond Franklin Roosevelt's program in the vain hope that this will cure the very problems government helped create. 2. We can seek to bring government under control and make it more manageable—to streamline government agencies, cut waste and duplication and keep a tight check on spending schemes. 3. We can turn toward a true free enterprise system through an "Age of Reform and Repeal," step by step ridding ourselves of those programs, policies, and ideas that have ended in impoverishing the poor and prosperous alike—programs instituted by government which contribute to the violation of individual rights, and deny the spirit and letter of the U.S. Constitution and Declaration of Independence. Because we have broken with these moral and philosophical covenants we are paying a heavy price in mounting chaos.

For those Americans who cherish freedom, the third course of action is the only avenue left open. Embarking on an "Age of Reform and Repeal" would mean removing the restraints that force freedom into a series of retreats and progressively limit the choice of the individual—a choice that our young people say they seek and which they accuse adults of frustrating.

The late Bernard Baruch, at ninety-three, offered the most salient advice for our troubled times when he stated:

> The role of government and its relationship to the individual has changed so radically that today government is involved in almost every aspect of our lives.
> Political, economic, and racial forces have developed which we have not yet learned to understand or control. If we are ever to master these forces, make certain that government will belong to the people, not the people to the government, and provide for the future better than the past, we must somehow learn from the experiences of the past."[183]

What we witness in today's troubled times are the tragic consequences of our revolt from our past and from proven moral principles, evidenced in our nation's college campuses becoming battlegrounds, and violently and vividly demonstrated during the Democratic Convention in Chicago in August 1968. In turning away from the true American tradition of reason, liberty, and law, we have turned away from reality itself—the reality characterized by a clear and consistent view of how society secures freedom and progress. Yet almost two hundred years ago a small group of remarkable men became the pathfinders for freedom and showed future generations the way to this reality.

It is our crucial responsibility to fashion a freedom manifesto for our troubled times; a practical program that begins to put America back on the track toward a free future. We shall overcome our troubled times if we but have the will and the intelligence to shape a realistic manifesto that reflects the principles, hopes, and highest expectations of our Founding Fathers, finishing what they so nobly began.

---

[183] Bernard Baruch, The New York *Times* (May 11, 1964).

XXII
The Great Political Riot : A Turning Point
in Time

The Founding Fathers of America realized that they
lived in an orderly universe. They recognized that all
existence was structured according to certain principles
which they called the laws of nature, and that the
human mind was capable of comprehending nature. . . .
They sought to harmonize their social system with the
system of the universe. They sought to harmonize the
laws of men with the laws of nature.[184] [Edmund
Contoski in *The Manifesto Of Individualism.*]

The Constitution of 1789 abundantly reflected the attempt to achieve harmony by offering a people an instrument
for political, social, and economic concord. Mistakes are certainly there. But on the whole, the emphasis of the Founders
on the need for harmony in human affairs as the keynote to
progress is matched by nature's insistence on harmony, and
on the natural punishment of all things that disturb or disrupt the natural order of things.

The Democratic Convention in Chicago in August 1968
demonstrated great disharmony, violence, and conflict. It is a
superb example of how far we have come from the concepts
of the Founders: to the belief that progress is only achieved
through conflict, tension, and social turmoil. The premise of
American political life beginning with the New Deal was that
force, by Government, was a proper instrument for achieving
progress; those who believe in this premise are now bewildered to find that the basic concept, in more brutal forms,
has extended itself to the streets of our cities, to our college
campuses, and, with the violent events in Chicago, to our
very political process. Political life in America, especially in
those urban centers controlled by New Deal-type political
machines, has operated on the assumption that society is
made up of conflicting groups to be played off one against
the other—management against labor, the public against the

[184]*Manifesto of Individualism* (New York; Exposition Press, 1968), p.
45.

private sector, producer against consumer, rich against poor, and now black against white. It has been wholly predictable that such a political philosophy should produce the nightmare social conflict we have today.

Convention Crucial Turning Point

It would be a tragic mistake, as we mean to illustrate in this work, to disregard the fuller meaning of Chicago. It was a turning point in the forward thrust of a radical and revolutionary movment in America which had been building since the early 1960s. These revolutionaries and radicals mean to take the nation's social, political, and economic system beyond the Socialistic programs of Franklin Roosevelt. We have pinpointed that those who went to Chicago to disrupt and discredit a major political party did so with the eventual goal of taking that party over and transforming it from a Liberal organization to something more radical and revolutionary than it has been in the past. Some of the most prominent political, moral, and intellectual leaders, in their desire to come to power, have been or still are willing to give monetary and moral support to such radicals and revolutionaries. And in the response of those law-and-order Liberals, within and without the party, suggests their incapacity to cope with these destructive forces. As a result, the Democratic Party may be allowed to drift to the radical Left. Aiding in this drift are those members of the mass media and men like Daniel Walker, who understand nothing of the tactics of these radicals and revolutionaries who are seeking to expand a political philosophy that is but a skeleton subsisting on the weight of its own deficiencies.

Just as the Liberal philosophy made possible the rise of radicalism, so it is likely that Liberals will become the "tools" of those revolutionaries who seek to destroy what remains of the free political, economic, and social system which the Revolution of 1776 made possible. The process by which this can come about was violently illustrated in Chicago. Many Liberals, for example, sided with the street radicals after the confrontation with the police—not wanting to recognize that the radicals went to Chicago with the intention of fomenting a "political riot" as a weapon to polarize opinion to their side and against the City and the Democratic Party. In the heat of emotion, and in the lack of a clear picture of the precise origins of "guerrilla insurrection," many Liberals became the tools of radicals and helped in advancing the cause of revolution in America.

The August 1968 Democratic Convention in Chicago was a crucial turning point in the political history of the United States. Prior to the 1968 Convention, violence initiated by the New Left had left our political process largely untouched. But in only one week in late August, violence was initiated and injected into the national political decision-making process. As a result, just as the student riots at the University of California at Berkeley in 1964 set the stage for other campus upheavals through the employment of physical force, the precedent set at the 1968 Convention could very well serve as a model in other areas of American political life.

Equally disturbing, the Great Political Riot of August 1968 was engineered by a mere handful of radicals, aided not by the poor and uneducated—but by middle-class youth educated in some of the most esteemed Liberal institutions of learning in the nation. Unaware of the all-important fact that initiation of physical force for moral and political objectives is suicidal for a free society, the well-educated middle-class young who joined the mob in the streets of Chicago were only extending in more violent terms the techniques that had begun during the civil rights movement of the early 1960s, and which their teachers and adult intellectual, political, and moral leaders had sanctioned.

What further extension of this principle we will witness in the years ahead, now that violence has invaded the political decision-making process, remains the least considered but most crucial question of the week of revolutionary warfare in Chicago.

The Warnings We Ignored

Perhaps the most crucial issue both the media and the political, intellectual, and moral leadership ignored when commenting on the Convention violence was that the roots of the Great Political Riot lie in the organization of the National Conference for New Politics in the summer of 1965 at the Center for the Study of Democratic Institutions. Possessing a predisposed bias in favor of the radicals, although unwilling to go as far in violent action, many members of the mass media and of the political world, opposed to then President Johnson, encouraged and supported the New Left. By refusing to see the probable consequence of New Left violence initiated in the name of opposition to the Vietnam War and to LBJ, men and women who should have known better offered active encouragement to the growth of a revolutionary movement bent on using mob rule to paralyze and destroy a free nation—in the name of creating something better than freedom.

The prediction this author and his associate Williamson Good made prior to the 1968 Democratic Convention was based on a hard-headed assessment of the philosophy and motivation of the New Left, and on the charting of its growth from Berkeley in 1964 to the Great Political Riot of August 1968. We understood the need of the New Left to perpetuate itself with more daring and dangerous acts of violence. This is in the tradition of revolutionary movements, which shift from one tactical issue to another as a means of achieving upward mobility. Understanding this, when the Pentagon March of October 1967 was staged, it took little thought to see that the radicals' activities at such gatherings as the September 1967 National Conference for New Politics Convention in Chicago were but one more step on the escalator to revolution. When men talk and applaud violence, it is not unreasonable to assume that they are priming themselves and working up the courage to actively use violence. As a result, especially when the October 1967 March gave way to early planning for the Great Political Riot ten months later, no one need have been surprised or shocked when violence exploded at the Democratic Convention.

But a review of the comments on the Convention by non-radicals and nonrevolutionaries revealed either an appalling ignorance of the clear warnings and preludes to Chicago, or a cynicism and cunning of men who had not the courage to initiate violence, but would stand on the sidelines and encourage or applaud such actions. The latter without question represented a small fraction of the mass of "outraged" comments over the Convention. For the majority of those who sided with the street radicals, emotional and ill-conceived notions about the real nature and origins of the disruptors ensured the "howling success" that the Great Political Riot became for Hayden, Dellinger, Davis, and others.

Ensuring the Success of Subversion

When men confronted with a crisis situation of the character of that which engulfed the Chicago Convention evade or ignore what has happened prior—The Pentagon March, the

1968 New York Grand Central Yip-In, Columbia University riots, for example—they disarm themselves to deal effectively with a similar crisis. When, however, men know they are the intended victims of a planned offensive, but evade that knowledge—it is a far greater moral crime than not knowing at all. Essentially, the evidence suggests very strongly that while the Liberal Democratic leadership knew what was planned for Chicago, they evaded the necessary thinking and planning to expose it beforehand because they believed to do so would both split the party and make them look bad in the eyes of the press and the public. In short, Mayor Richard Daley and the Democratic leaders believed that pursuing a course of action that played down the threat would somehow allow them to muddle through. But, as the course of events vividly illustrated, the pursuit of this "see-no-evil" policy only worsened the disaster for both Daley and the law-and-order Democrats. Equally crucial in discrediting the case of the city of Chicago were its own actions such as making an issue of the park, and its lack of a sophisticated understanding of what the radicals were seeking to stage-manage. In the pursuit of a policy of "compromise" with those out to destroy and discredit the Convention and Chicago's political administration, and in their over-reaction, the necessary basis was formed for ensuring the success of the revolutionaries and radicals who went to Chicago. In misapplying the necessary police force to contain the confrontation in the park and in front of the Hilton, the City only reinforced the false image it had allowed to build up for weeks in advance—that Chicago was a city that relied on "nightstick repression." If, however, the city had made its case very early—setting forth the facts as to the radical meetings going back to 1967, the trips of the ttroublemakers to Communist countries, and the secret meetings days prior to the Convention—it would have disarmed those hostile in the press and in the Democratic Party. But it waited until almost the start of the Convention to make its case, which by then seemed self-serving. The lack of even an intelligent exposition of its side of the story in its later report and TV program only reinforced the belief in the minds of the press and other anti-Chicago factions that this was merely an attempt to justify "police brutality."

This set of circumstances is not dissimilar to the statements and actions of university and political leaders who have sought to deal with the earlier disorders of the 1960s.

Fundamentally, the causes of these official failures stem from two areas. First, early concession of key issues to those seeking violent confrontation gives official sanction to mob violence. In the case of Chicago, this is apparent in the willingness of the city to believe that the radicals were talking in good faith and would make their demonstrations nonviolent. Second, failure to understand fully the New Left from a philosophical, intellectual, and strategic point of view gives the radicals an enormous advantage. Most officials forced to deal with the New Left still think of demonstrations as in the character of the early civil rights movement; they would better be studying the history of revolutionary movements prior to both World Wars, and the writings of New Left heroes like Che Guevera, Fidel Castro, and others, for some clue as to how to deal intelligently with demonstrations calculated to ignite violence for political ends.

In the final analysis, official failure and default in the face of New Left extremism is the product of a lethal contradiction held by modern Liberalism: the contradictory beliefs in the force of government on one hand and in freedom on the other. Such contradictory thinking has, since the FDR New Deal, encouraged progressive use of force and has sent individual freedom into a series of retreats. The failure of officials in Chicago to deal decisively with violent assault on the political process was the end result of this contradiction: bewildered officials unwittingly shared with the radicals certain basic and important premises. The difference is that the radicals, having fully abandoned peaceful persuasion, freedom, and reason in favor of physical force to settle political questions, confronted officials at the Convention with an uncompromising stance, while Daley and others assumed, as in the past, some accommodation by appeasement of force could be worked out. Bewildered and confused at this ruthless radical consistency, blinded by their own unwillingness to see the real goals of the radicals, and incapable of shaping a strategy that would intelligently meet the most serious crisis confronting the American political scene since the Civil War, they surrendered by default to the triumph of mob rule over reason, freedom, and the peaceful political process.

The Men Who Make Mobs Possible

The dangerous self-disarmament of Democratic Party officials in dealing with the Convention crisis is nowhere near as disgraceful and shameful as that of the disruptive delegates inside the Convention, the mass media who sided with those inside and outside the Convention, and individuals such as Senator Eugene McCarthy. In focusing the blame on Daley and the city of Chicago, the radical delegates, the media, and McCarthy were, consciously or unconsciously, serving to destroy the Democratic process. It is nothing less than the worst kind of intellectual evasion or dishonesty for the media to have ignored the role the disruptive delegates played in making mob rule in Chicago possible; or to have completely disregarded the clear link between those inside the Convention and those in the streets, and the abundant and irrefutable evidence of premeditation on the part of both groups that dates back almost a year.

The special shame of McCarthy is the least appreciated factor in making the Great Political Riot a howling success for the revolution. McCarthy, despite his pleas for his supporters to stay away from Chicago a week before the Convention, could have and should have acted to prevent his idealistic and youthful supporters from being used in a cynical radical ploy that resulted in the injury of many and, in their subsequent disillusionment, with a political process that was far—at least then—from being as corrupt as they have come to believe it is. McCarthy showed a total disregard for his own youthful supporters, and for the very Democratic process he regularly claimed his campaign was inspired to save, by standing in the park that Thursday afternoon and virtually sanctioning the brute force with entreaties to help "seize the party." In not condemning the premeditation to foment a riot, he gave moral sanction to the New Left to continue its dirty business of using force for political objectives. As author and critic Diana Trilling is quoted earlier as saying, McCarthy, in not denouncing New Left actions that brought about the use of the police, bowed to the New Left revolutionary notion that Liberalism "has no move to make except to dissolve into the arms of the revolution."[185]

Members of the mass media, in not presenting a balanced and accurate picture of what happened in Chicago and why, played a crucial role in aiding and abetting the aims of the New Left. Their predisposed bias is to their great discredit, and only widens the growing gulf between the media and the

---

[185] Diana Trilling, *op. cit.*

reading and viewing public it pretends to serve. The media's coverage of Chicago demonstrated a particular kind of intellectual corruptness in those who control and program the media, especially TV. It is a corruptness born of the firmly held belief that its members possess an intellectual and moral superiority about the shape of social policy, which an uninformed majority is incapable of determining. While much of the media is dominated by Liberalism, this is clearly in contradiction with the stated Liberal principle of Democratic majority rule. And in the case of Chicago—according to a nationwide opinion poll and the volume of mail received by Daley which came in five to one in his favor—the majority of Americans thought that Daley did the right thing, irrespective of his reasons, and that mass media turned in one of the shabbiest jobs of reporting in recent history.[186] It would, incidentally, be a different story if the mistakes of the media in Chicago were merely the result of misinformation, and were happening for the first time. This is just not the case. The media has been responsible for helping to create a national political revolutionary movement by its unbalanced coverage of the violent events that preceded Chicago, beginning with the 1964 Berkeley upheaval, the urban riots, the college disruption, and right through to the Pentagon March. The coverage of Chicago demonstrated not just what Liberal columnist Joseph Kraft termed a "systematic bias," but a failure to understand fully the severity of the crisis and of the destructive forces they have helped to unleash on a free society.

As a consequence, when the Walker Report was released (not to forget the manner and method used to bring it to the public's attention), the clear implication was that Chicago's was a "police riot," a phrase that has gained great currency in absolving the men who made mob rule in Chicago possible. Given so many unwilling or unable to see that Chicago 1968 was a low number in the countdown to chaos, it is not surprising that neither Daley, the mass media, McCarthy, nor the Walker Report could even glimpse what the events in Chicago

---

[186] According to Reuters, September 5, 1968, the million member International Association of Machinists and Aerospace Workers endorsed and complimented Mayor Daley for his conduct and action. And columnist Kay Gardella reported, ". . . all of the mail received by this department from viewers was 100 percent against the TV coverage," New York *Daily News*, (September 5, 1968).

meant for the future of a free and representative political system in America.

Blind Liberals Leading the Blind

Unable to see that the political riot was the natural outcome of what had gone before, it was no surprise that liberals would be unable to speculate on what could happen to America in the second half of this century if the radical premises acted on in Chicago gain wider acceptance, especially among the young. In order to make such a projection, such Liberals would have to acknowledge, as did Gus Tyler, that the battle in Chicago was a glimpse of what the future could become if the New Left succeeds, and that it was a "miniature preview of the nation's fate should the polarization of politics proceed in the U.S.";[187] or, that the New Left draws inspiration for its revolutionary movement from the events in Russia prior to 1905 and, as Irving Howe observed, that the actions of the New Left in its politics of confrontation "could lead to a major crisis for democracy"[188] not unlike that which gripped Germany prior to Hitler. Howe also wrote of setting precedents for using violence as a political weapon, which was one of the major aims of the New Left in Chicago; to accustom men to the idea that it is both right and desirable to use brute force to solve political questions. To evade or dismiss the German experience of the 1920s is to miss the point set forth by British observer and journalist Peregrine Worsthorne that "sizable groups of the German middle class lost faith in democracy,"[189] just as the disruptive delegates and middle-class McCarthy supporters did.

One could concede that the danger is very real, but deny that the forces are present in America to carry the political, social, and economic system to more destructive and potentially dictatorial forms. But as illustrated by the actions, statements, and program of the New Left, it is very much dedicated to the idea of using violence and disruption to carry the nation beyond the welfare state. And as New Democratic Coalition ally Michael Harrington has clearly spelled out, the country has no choice since Liberalism can-

---

[187]"The Liberal Crisis—Now," *The New Leader* (October 7, 1968).

[188]"The New 'Confrontation Politics' Is a Dangerous Game," *The New York Times Magazine* (October 20, 1968).

[189]London *Sunday Telegraph* (September 1, 1968).

not respond "to challenges unless it moves sharply to the Democratic left" and in the process "go beyond Franklin Roosevelt."[190]

Chicago and the Crucial Connection

If we are to profit from the stern lessons and warnings Chicago and other violent events offer, we should not make the mistake of assuming that behind the premeditation to foment a political riot were not specific goals—to push the nation into a serious political, economic, and social crisis by a series of "Chicagos" leading to violent revolution. We must not ignore, too, the factors in the past which created a similar crisis in Europe which led to Communism flourishing in one place, Nazism in another, and Facism in still another.

The welfare state in Europe, prior to both World Wars, became the bridgehead to the police or total state. Prior to the rise of dictatorship in Europe earlier in this century, a few warned of the "coming slavery." Herbert Spencer warned his own generation in 1884; George Orwell has offered a warning for our own time in *1984*. The prelude to each dictatorship significantly included the collapse of Liberalism and the downfall of well-meaning men who believed in force and freedom at the same time, and with it the disintegration of the welfare state systems and the rise of radical and revolutionary forces who used street violence for achieving political objectives. In each case, the spark that set off European revolutions that led to dictatorship was the uprising of the young, which began—as it has in America—in the universities and spread to society as a whole. And for our own times, the observation of Brooklyn College Professor Dr. Leonard Peikoff is sobering and ominous: that the time span between the Bismarck Welfare State and Hitler's National Socialism was forty-five years; between the election of the FDR New Deal and the 1968 Great Political Riot was thirty-five years.

In root terms what made the New Deal possible was the intellectual and philosophical currents of thought that began germinating in the American university system shortly after the U.S. Civil War and represented a counterrevolutionary force against the philosophy, principles, and political program of the Founders. We can see a direct relationship and concurrent thread of influence between the American Fabian

---

[190]Michael Harrington, *op. cit.*

Socialists and Marxists of the latter nineteenth century and today's New Left. Thorstein Veblen influenced Rexford Tugwell with his Marxist dogma and Tugwell today influences New Left students who would wage all-out revolution in completing the political program of the New Deal—which Tugwell had a hand in shaping in the 1930s. As we have illustrated by Tugwell's own words, his own view of the future, shared by many like him in the intellectual and political world, involves the enactment of a new constitution—after decades of seeking to subvert or violate the U.S. Constitution of 1789. It is this document that stands like a philosophical rock of Gibraltar, in the way of those radicals and revolutionaries who seek the total power of the State over the individual in America.

It is this set of circumstances that makes the violent events in Chicago, indeed the violence of the entire "sick Sixties," a warning that we ignore at our own peril and at that of future generations.

Whether we survive as a free, prosperous, and secure people, will depend in large measure on whether we learn from the mistakes of the past—be we genuine law-and-order, reason-oriented Liberals or Conservatives. We need to have a clearer understanding of the principles and political program that produced the remarkable American Republic; an understanding of the fuller meaning of the American, Industrial and Technological Revolutions. In viewing this triple revolution of the last two hundred years in its true perspective, we may come to appreciate the fact that the violence of the 1960s is the direct result of allowing the intent of 1776 and 1789 to be interrupted. If once we come firmly to this conviction, we may proceed to adopt policies that will lead toward finishing the work of the Founders—policies which provide the moral cement for a genuinely free and humane society.

And, to this end, we need real revolutionaries in the spirit of the Founders, a role best suited to young people who are now adrift in a sea of uncertainty, without moral and philosophical guidance. They have no well-defined way of finding out just what are the philosophical and political principles the Founders embraced, the principles that caused a continent to be transformed from a wilderness to a world power within the shortest period of time in the entire history of mankind.

The current stagnant course proposed by New Deal Liberalism is not the answer to the crisis confronting America, since it is first and foremost a philosophical, moral, and intellectual crisis that Liberalism made possible. Nor is it the answer to accept the program of the New Left, which Liberalism gave birth to and which vows to carry us to more extreme forms that would concentrate power in the hands of the few over the many. The only course left to America in the second half of this century, as we approach the two hundredth anniversary of the signing of the Declaration of Independence, is that of finishing the work of the Founders, of creating a genuinely free and open society based upon law, liberty, and the philosophy of reason.

It is little appreciated that of all the revolutionary upheavals of the last two centuries the only truly successful revolution was in America. In this regard, after a lifetime of studying and writing aabout the history of Western civilization, the historians Will and Ariel Durant came to some basic conclusions of what the past offers as a guide to the future. In *The Lessons of History,* the Durants tell us that sooner or later every social, political system must come to adopt some form of incentives and rewards if progress is to be achieved; competition by harmonious, reasoned concord forms the biology of history and offers the best guidelines for potential greatness for a nation. As to violent revolutions, including the one sought by the New Left in "confrontations" like Chicago, the Durants concluded the following:

> Violent revolutions do not so much redistribute the wealth as destroy it. There may be a redivision of land, but the natural inequality of men soon recreates an inequality of possessions and privileges. The only real revolution is in the enlightenment of the mind and the improvement of the human character. The only real emancipation is individual and the only real revolutionists are philosophers and saints.[191]

We must become real revolutionaries in the tradition of the signers of the Declaration of Independence; they were not timid men who founded our republic, and timid men will not preserve, protect, or strengthen it.

---

[191] Will and Ariel Durant, *op.cit.*

APPENDIX I

The following is excerpted from The Strategy of Confrontation: Chicago and the Democratic National Convention, *a report put out by the City of Chicago on September 6, 1968.*

INTRODUCTION

From the beginning of 1968, the Democratic National Convention was "D" Day for many dissident groups in the United States. The most obvious efforts were those of the National Mobilization Committee and the Youth International Party. Plans were made to disrupt the National Convention and paralyze the City of Chicago. The plans were announced publicly, training for the encounter was carried on publicly, and the attempt to disrupt was openly launched.

Responsible governmental agencies noted the plans and preparations and took the appropriate measures necessary to cope with the promised attack. Members of the 12,000 man Police Department were placed on twelve hour duty rather than the normal eight hour tour of duty; the Illinois National Guard was activated and readied in case of emergency at the Armories within the City; and Federal troops, who never entered the City, were conveniently located in readiness at O'Hare and Glenview air stations.

Psychological warfare was waged by the dissidents for weeks in Chicago and several outbreaks of actual violence did occur during the Convention week of August 25-30, 1968—the most serious being the incident which occurred in front of the Hilton Hotel on August 28 from 7:57 P.M. to 8:15 P.M.

Although publicity, largely unfavorable, was enormous, arrests and injuries were moderate. The Convention was not disrupted; the City was not paralyzed. Not one shot was fired; not one life lost.

Now, as a natural aftermath of recent events, we enter into the period of assessment of the performance of governmental officials, police and military units, radio, television and newspapers. Toward this end and in an effort to begin to detail

what happened in Chicago during the Convention Week, we
have prepared this report.

BACKGROUND OF EVENTS LEADING TO CONVENTION

On October 8, 1967, the National Democratic Committee
announced that Chicago had been selected to be the site for
the Democratic National Convention scheduled for August
26th through 29th, 1968.

It soon became apparent that thousands of delegates and
newsmen, plus families and friends, were not the only ones
planning to visit Chicago that week. As far back as November
16, 1967, *The Village Voice* reported the leader of the Youth
International Party, Jerry Rubin, as saying "See you next
August in Chicago at the Democratic National Convention.
Bring pot, fake delegates' cards, smoke bombs, costumes,
blood to throw and all kinds of interesting props. Also football helmets."[1]

Early in 1968 the National Mobilization Committee Against
the War in Vietnam headed by David Dellinger organized a Chicago Project Committee and placed Rennie Davis in charge
with instructions to work closely with Tom Hayden, leader of
Students for a Democratic Society and Jerry Rubin, head of
the Progressive Labor Party and also of the Youth International
Party, more commonly known as Yippies. All had previously
cooperated in the march on the Pentagon in October of 1967.
Many other, less prominent militants from other groups were
also invited to a meeting on March 24, 1968, at the Y. M. C. A.
camp near Lake Villa to coordinate plans. It was announced
that some 85 organizations were scheduled to move into Chicago for the "battle of the century".[2]

Dellinger and Hayden held a press conference in New York
on June 29th and were quoted by the magazine *Guardian* as
saying, "We are planning tactics of prolonged direct action to
put heat on the government and its political party. We realize
that it will be no picnic but responsibility for any violence that
develops lies with the authorities, not the demonstrators."

Barron's which reported the interview explained that:

> "In New Left rhetoric 'direct action' can include
> street barricading, fire bombing, seizure of buildings and
> massive confrontations with the police . . . Hayden

---

[1] *The Village Voice*—November 16, 1967.
[2] *Saga Magazine*—August 6, 1968

means, of course, that Chicago police must not stop his shock troops if they invade the convention hall, block traffic, or make exits and entrances impossible. Such tactics, refined at Columbia were tested first at the Pentagon . . . ten of the 'peace protesters' actually managed to penetrate the Pentagon. With their ranks greatly swelled in Chicago, how many more might gain access to the convention floor, even physically taking it over? More than a hundred anti-war groups mustered for the march on the Pentagon produced a mob force estimated at 55,000. For Chicago that number easily could double or triple. On June 29, both Dellinger and Hayden stated that most of the organizations present at the Pentagon will return for the Convention. The Yippies marshalled 5,000 at Grand Central . . . All told, the motley crowd converging on Chicago could number a quarter-million."[3]

The *Saturday Evening Post* commented:

"The anti-war protest movement promises to bring tens of thousands of demonstrators—mostly young students—into the city. According to present plans, the crowds will build to a climax at the time of the nomination, when they will surround the meeting site with a 'sea of people'. . . . Their presence could trigger the discontent of Chicago's own slum residents . . ."[4]

Local newspapers carried almost daily stories enlarging on protest plans and detailing ways that dissidents could make it unpleasant and even impossible for the Convention to transact its business. Richard Strout writing in the *Christian Science Monitor* observed:

"The news media in this city may be indicted for inciting to violence. The mildest parade of young people brings a TV camera crew like a hook-and-ladder truck to a three alarm fire. Any youngster who will denounce the authorities finds himself surrounded by a ring of extended microphones. The press has talked so much about violence that it has a vested interest in violence. It will look silly if it doesn't get it. This is a case where "the medium is the message'."[5]

---

[3] Barron's National Business & Financial Weekly—August 19, 1968. "Ballots or Bullets" by William Good and Jeffrey St. John.

[4] Saturday Evening Post—August 24, 1968. "Can the Ringmaster Keep the Show Going" by Milton Viorst—Page 26.

[5] Christian Science Monitor—August. "News Media 'prepare' Chicago for Violence" by Richard L. Strout.

Meanwhile the Chicago Police, in cooperation with the Secret Service and the Federal Bureau of Investigation were collecting additional intelligence. At a July 13 meeting at National Mobilization Committee Headquarters, 407 S. Dearborn, over which Rennie Davis presided, plans were revealed by the National Mobilization Committee to bring in 100,000 protesters to the Convention; also tie up two Army divisions and make surface transportation to the Convention site impossible.[6]

On August 9, leaders Rennie Davis, Tom Hayden and others met with Abbie Hoffman, Yippie organizer, to discuss plans for demonstrating during the Convention. Classes in street fighting and guerrilla tactics taught by Hoffman were scheduled to begin on August 20 and strategy to force the Police Department to spread itself over a large area laid.

Early in August, Rennie Davis appeared before a meeting of the Chicago Peace Council held at the Lawson YMCA. He displayed two large 3' by 3' maps of the area surrounding the International Amphitheater, noting locations where police, National Guard, FBI and other security forces would be situated during the proceedings. He stated that if trouble starts at the Democratic National Convention, among other things "the loop will fall" implying the demolition of the downtown Chicago area.[7] Fourteen "Primary Targets" [were] listed. . . .

Private citizens and newspaper reporters did, as a matter of fact, witness the training carried on by Hoffman and others. Snake dancing, defensive blocking, kicking of adversary in leg or groin were demonstrated and practiced during the "Marshals" training. Use of red or green flares as weapons, also oven cleaning spray, hair spray and manufacture of primitive but effective missiles such as nails stuck into golf balls, razors concealed in canes and darts made from sharpened coat hangers was also part of the instruction. . . . stores near Lincoln Park report[ed] unusual sale of caustic materials. . . . All potential participants in the demonstrations were advised to try to be photographed while being arrested and several demonstrators arrested carried lists of telephone numbers of local and national news media. Violence in this situation was inevitable, expected and even sought. The demonstrators organized their own "first aid units" and also conducted practice with these "medics".

[6]Intelligence Division Report—Chicago Police Department—July 15, 1968.
[7]Intelligence Division Report—Chicago Police Department—August 12, 1968.

They were in contact with a "Committee of 100 Lawyers" to give them legal assistance in case of arrest and spoke of a bail bond fund.

Incredible as it may sound in the light of later occurrences, the August 9th Intelligence Division Report of the Chicago Police Department concludes:

"Due to the talk around the office of the National Mobilization Committee and the general attitude of Rennie Davis and Tom Hayden, the reporting investigator feels that the night of 28 August 1968 there will be wide-spread trouble through efforts of Davis and Hayden. It is felt that there will be trouble in the Loop area and possibly on the South and West Sides. This would be done in an effort to draw the Police away from the Amphitheatre."[8]

Of a different, but equally menacing type, were the plans arriving to Police Intelligence of schemes to assassinate Senator Eugene McCarthy, Vice President Hubert Humphrey, Mayor Richard J. Daley and other political and civic leaders. Perhaps the most unnerving rumor was one of a plan to murder a young female supporter of Senator Eugene McCarthy and blame it on the police. The police did not want to publicize any of these plots and rumors of plots for fear of planting the idea in still other minds.[9]

BIOGRAPHICAL NOTES REGARDING RADICAL LEADERS

The following notes[10] give some background on a few of the principals who were involved in confrontation with law enforcement authorities during the week of August 25 to August 30, 1968. These biographical sketches show that they are not strangers to the tactics of confrontation, having been involved in many of the recent mass disorders extending from Berkeley to Columbia to the Pentagon. The outline shows travel to communist countries, draft evasion and disregard for orderly process of dissent.

---

[8]*Ibid.*

[9]Intelligence Division Report—Chicago Police Department—August 20, 1968.—These threats coming as they did upon the heels of the assassinations of President John F. Kennedy, Rev. Dr. Martin Luther King, Jr., and Robert F. Kennedy, such reports deservedly required more than perfunctory treatment. A Federal Grand Jury probe was initiated by the United States Attorney's Office in regard to this matter.

[10]Compiled from reports contained in the office of the Chicago Police Department and the Federal Bureau of Investigation.

Rennie Davis

Rennard (Rennie) Cordon Davis served as local Coordinator of the National Mobilization Committee. He is a chief planner of the Center for Radical Research, a radical left-wing organization; an organizer of Resistance Inside the Army (RITA), which has as its purpose the subversion of military personnel within the Army; and actively engaged in the program of Students for Democratic Society (SDS), a radical left-wing organization. Davis, during the month of November, 1967, visited North Vietnam at the invitation of the Hanoi government.

Tom Hayden

Thomas (Tom) E. Hayden is an organizer and former Secretary of the Students for a Democratic Society. He is also an organizer of a group known as the Newark Community Project which was very active during the Newark, New Jersey riots which took place on July 12 through July 17 of 1967. Hayden was referred to by newspapers in New Jersey as the "Maoist Messiah from Michigan." He served behind the scenes at the Columbia University riots and rebellion. Hayden has also visited Hanoi in North Vietnam, against United States policy. His encounters with police in Chicago included resisting arrest and battery on August 27, 1968, obstructing police officers and resisting arrest and disorderly conduct on August 26, 1968. He is considered among the "hip" movement as a violent revolutionary.

Abbie Hoffman

Abbie Hoffman is one of the organizers of the Youth International Party (Yippies). He served as a coordinator of the proposed Festival of Life to be sponsored by the Yippies during the Convention. On May 9, 1968, Hoffman advised a meeting of the Students for Democratic Society of his involvement in the disorders at Columbia University. On May 18, 1967 Hoffman participated in the Washington Square Park (in New York City) march to protest alleged police brutality and to prove that "the streets belong to the people." On November 25, 1967, Hoffman sponsored another demonstration marching from Washington Square Park to Times Square and then to the United Nations in New York, a march alleged to have been conducted by a group known as PTA (Protesters, Terrorists and Anarchists).

Jerry Rubin

Another Yippie leader who devoted his time and talent to

bring disruption in the City during the Democratic National Convention was Jerry Rubin. Rubin is a member of the National Coordinating Committee to end the war in Vietnam, which is Communist infiltrated. Rubin visited Cuba during 1964. He attended and was arrested for participating in a demonstration against General Maxwell Taylor on August 24, 1965. He was also arrested for disorderly conduct in Washington, D.C. on August 19, 1966, and in Oakland, California for criminal trespass on November 30, 1966. He was convicted in the student sit-in at the University of California in Berkeley on January 28, 1967. On August 28, 1968, he was arrested at Madison and Dearborn Streets for having led a large group of Yippies who had entered the downtown area and commenced throwing trash cans and garbage into the streets.

David Dellinger

David Dellinger is Chairman of the National Mobilization Committee. He was convicted in 1939 and 1943 for violations of the Selective Service Laws. Dellinger was jailed for ten days by the Washington D.C. police, in a demonstration against the Central Intelligence Agency in 1961. He visited Cuba during the May Day Celebrations in 1964. Dellinger was arrested during a demonstration of the "Assembly of Unrepresented People to Declare Peace in Vietnam" held in Washington D.C. in 1965. He also visited North Vietnam in 1967 contrary to United States policy. He is alleged to have admitted being a Communist.

ATTEMPTS TO ACCOMMODATE DISSIDENT GROUPS

Meetings in Mayor's Office

In spite of the unpopular views espoused by the dissident groups and the notorious background of their leaders, the City of Chicago sought to protect their constitutional rights of freedom of assembly and freedom of speech. Meetings were held with officers and representatives of the Youth International Party and the National Mobilization Committee to end the war in Vietnam. In the office of the Mayor, several meetings were held in which David Stahl, Mayor's Administrative Officer, Raymond F. Simon, Corporation Counsel and Richard Elrod, Assistant Corporation Counsel, participated.

At these meetings, it was pointed out that all of the public facilities in the City of Chicago would be available to members of the "Yippies" and "MOB," so long as they were used in a peaceful, orderly and lawful manner. It was pointed out that plans could not be approved for members to sleep in the parks since park ordinances of long standing prohibit the use of parks after 11:00 P.M. In regard to routes of march and places of assembly, the City's position indicated that the area immediately adjacent to the International Amphitheater could not be used for a mass assembly of persons because of security preparations of federal and local authorities. An invitation to submit plans for marches and assemblies which would not conflict with these security precautions was made and continuously reiterated.

Meetings in Chambers
Hon. Wm. J. Lynch, U.S. District Court
Nonetheless, suit was filed in the United States District Court by the National Mobilization Committee.[11] On Wednesday, August 21, 1968, extensive discussions were held in the chambers of the United States District Court Judge William Lynch. During these discussions the City of Chicago pointed out its willingness to accommodate any reasonable march which was desired by the National Mobilization Committee. The following specific proposals were made by the Corporation Counsel, Raymond F. Simon, and are part of the official proceedings.[12]

1. A march from the Monroe Street Parking Lot at Monroe and Columbus Drive, south to the band shell at 11th Street and Columbus Drive in Grant Park.

2. A march from the parking lot at McCormick Place, northbound along the Outer Drive to the band shell at Grant Park.

3. A march from Lake Shore Park located at Chicago Avenue and Lake Shore Drive, southbound along the Outer Drive to Jackson Boulevard, west on Jackson

---

[11]*National Mobilization Committee to End the War in Viet Nam, et al. v. Richard J. Daley, Mayor, et al.*, United States District Court for the Northern District of Illinois, 68 C 1528.

[12]The "confrontation" in court over parade permits which occurred on August 21 was filmed and witnessed by numerous TV stations. These interviews which showed the National Mobilization Committee and Youth International Party refusing all alternate parade routes offered by the authorities would have done much to ameliorate the criticism that the protesters had been offered no legitimate outlet. These films were never shown.

Boulevard to Columbus Drive and south on Columbus Drive to the band shell at Grant Park.

4. A march from Wacker Drive at Jackson Boulevard, eastward on Jackson Boulevard, through the loop to Columbus Drive and then south on Columbus Drive to the band shell at Grant Park.

Places proposed by the Corporation Counsel for holding assemblies included the Band Shell at Grant Park, an assembly at Burnham Park, Lincoln Park, Washington Park and Garfield Park. None of the offers, except an assembly on Wednesday, August 28, 1968, at Grant Park, were accepted. Throughout the negotiations, held in the United States District Court on August 21 and 22, the spokesman and attorney of the National Mobilization Committee continuously reiterated their insistence upon a meeting site within "eyeshot" of the Amphitheater. The parking lot located at 47th and Halsted Streets on the private property of the Community Discount Centers was sought. Upon inquiry, the Corporation Counsel was advised that it could not be made available because the Center would be open that evening and the area was needed for customer parking. This information was reported to the National Mobilization Committee in an open court session before Judge Lynch and is part of the official proceedings before the court. In addition to the location at the northwest corner of 47th and Halsted Streets, the Mobilization Committee indicated a desire to meet just west of the International Amphitheater. This also was private property and was not available. *No other specific request for an assembly area was made by the Mobilization Committee* in spite of repeated requests from the City for locations of any place where it would be reasonable to bring a large number of demonstrators.

Numbers Expected
The applications for parade and assembly permits signed by Rennie Davis (made part of the complaint in the lawsuit filed by the "MOB"), indicated that 200,000 persons would march to the Amphitheater on August 28, 1968. A second application indicated that 150,000 persons would march and assemble at the Amphitheater on August 28, 1968. The duration of the marches would be from 11:00 A.M. until 12 midnight. Another application requested the use of the Grant Park Band Shell for an assembly of 150,000 persons on August 28, 1968. In the light of these projected figures, traffic and security considera-

tions precluded any street rally point in the vicinity of the Amphitheater. The City stated that the purpose for wanting to march and assemble, which was ostensibly to point out criticisms of the country's policy in participating in the war in Vietnam, could be achieved by a march in the downtown area and an assembly at Chicago's famous Grant Park Band Shell.

The National Mobilization Committee suit was dismissed by United States District Court Judge William Lynch. In a similar lawsuit, the Youth International Party sought permission for "thousands of persons" to sleep in the public parks of Chicago, especially at Lincoln Park. This suit was dismissed by plaintiffs themselves.

Insistence Upon Amphitheatre

The position of the City that the rights of free speech and free assembly would be upheld and that any effort to march or assemble in a reasonable way would be accommodated by the City, were rejected by the continuous insistence by the Mobilization and Yippy organizations that they would march to the Amphitheater with or without permission, no other place being satisfactory. The appeals to assist the police of the City of Chicago and the security agencies of the federal government, appeals to avoid adding congestions to an already crowded area, were ignored. In dismissing the suit, Judge Lynch cited recent decisions of the United States Supreme Court, holding "that local governments are entitled to regulate the use of their streets and other public places [citations omitted] . . . The prevention of public disorder and violations are important objects of legitimate state concern when protest takes the form of mass demonstrations and parades [citation omitted] ". The court also cited the fact that numerous alternative routes and alternative places of public assembly had been suggested by the City of Chicago and Chicago Park District and concluded that the City and Park District acted in a reasonable and non-discriminatory manner. The court held that . . . "it would be a novel interpretation to hold that the First and Fourteenth Amendments require municipal government to provide a public park as sleeping accommodations for persons desiring to visit the City."

INJURIES SUSTAINED DURING CONVENTION WEEK

From the following information which relates to injuries which were sustained during the confrontations encountered during Convention Week in Chicago, it is interesting to note the large number of police officers who sustained injuries. The Police Department is presently investigating all complaints of excessive force which were lodged with the Department by newsmen and civilians who were injured during this week.

Police Officers

During the disturbances involving confrontations with dissidents, 198 Chicago Police Officers were injured—some seriously. National Guard personnel also suffered injuries during their tour of duty between August 25 and August 30. Many law enforcement officers received medical treatment for human bites, kicks in the groin, as well as from the weapons used and objects thrown by the dissidents. Other were injured, but saved from serious injury from bricks and sharp objects thrown at them only by their wearing of protective riot helmets.

Civilians

The partial survey of the Chicago Hospitals indicates that approximately 60 persons were treated at hospitals for injuries sustained during the course of the disorders. Some of these persons may be innocent victims injured by the dissidents themselves or injured by the police after being maneuvered into the front lines by the experienced agitators to force the confrontation.

Newsmen

An estimated 4,000 out-of-town newsmen came to Chicago to report the Democratic National Convention and surrounding events. Also in the City were 2,300 local newsmen who hold press cards issued by the Chicago Police Department.

During the period of the convention, complaints were made to the Department that 13 newsmen were assaulted by police officers. These complaints are being probed by the Internal Investigation Division. Also under investigation are 9 other allegations of attacks on newsmen which were reported in the press but not officially reported to the Police Department.

As of this date, none of these 22 investigations has been completed. Only 14 of the 22 newsmen have been available for statements. Many of the injured newsmen already have left Chicago and must be contacted by the I. I. D. in their home cities.

ARRESTED PERSONS

There were 641 arrested during the disorders of the week of

the Democratic National Convention. Of these, only 280 were under the age of 21. Only 208 were students. At the most, 175 were residents of the City of Chicago. The conclusion is inescapable: *An overwhelming majority of the persons arrested were not youngsters, were not students and were not Chicagoans.* They were adult trouble makers who came into the City of Chicago for the avowed purpose of a hostile confrontation with law enforcement.

Another noteworthy aspect relates to post-arrest procedures. There is no dispute that the processing of those persons arrested, including the setting of bail, availability of defense counsel, and Judges has been fair and speedy and within the guidelines of the "Kerner" and "Austin" Reports.

INCIDENTS AT CONVENTION HALL

Dan Rather

Mr. Rather was not struck by a Chicago police officer. He was struck by a private security guard at the Democratic National Convention (who claimed the incident was accidental). CBS has dropped the matter.

Mike Wallace

Mike Wallace admittedly grabbed the face of a Chicago Police Captain. The captain hit Wallace, allegedly in self-defense. After the incident, the participants shook hands and agreed to drop the matter.

David Hoeh, Delegate from New Hampshire

On August 29, 1968 at about 7:30 P.M. Mr. David Hoeh was taken into custody and detained for causing a disturbance at the extreme west delegate pass gate. Mr. Hoeh discovered that a credit card would activate the automatic delegate pass scanner. While attempting to give a public demonstration of this a remonstration was made by an Andy Frain usher which caused Mr. Hoeh to become loud and boisterous. Sgt. McCann of the Chicago Police Department was attracted to the disturbance but nothing could quiet Mr. Hoeh.

Mr. Hoeh began hollering and punching and kicking the investigating officers. He tore Sgt. McCann's star from his shirt and bit the finger of another officer. This injury was treated at Mercy Hospital. Mr. Hoeh suffered a slight scratch on his forehead some time during the melee.

Mr. Hoeh was handcuffed; removed from the Amphitheater

and taken to the 9th District Police Station in order that his status as a delegate could be evaluated. He was discovered to have 5 delegate passes.

Hoeh was released and driven back to the Amphitheater.

Hoeh has since been publicly criticized by a fellow New Hampshire delegate for his conduct at the National Convention.

PROBLEMS OCCASIONED BY THE STRATEGY OF CONFRONTATION

To Hold the Convention or Refuse It

The first problem proposed by the Politics of Confrontation was whether to advise the Convention, as a result of widely publicized threats to seek another site. Since the dissident groups intended to descend upon Chicago precisely because it *was* the Convention site, it would have actually solved nothing to refuse the Convention, except to shift the problem elsewhere. During the previous four months two of the nation's most outstanding men, the Rev. Martin Luther King, Jr. and Robert F. Kennedy had been assassinated in entirely different sections of the country. In this atmosphere any public gathering of prominent men constituted great risk. However, if the normal operation of our governmental processes were not to be halted by fear or submission to blackmail by threat, it seemed clear that Chicago should take proper precautions but proceed with the Convention.

Should Yippies Be Permitted to Sleep in the Park

The next specific decision which had to be made by city officials was the response to the request for permission to sleep in the parks. The City has had, and enforced, since 1940 an ordinance which prohibits citizens from sleeping or otherwise occupying the parks after 11 P.M.[19] In view of the fact that our local citizens, the taxpayers who maintain the parks, are not permitted to sleep in them and since the persons requesting this permission had openly announced their intention to disrupt our City and disturb our invited guests, it seemed doubly inadvisable to permit this unusual use. In addition, city departments of health, sanitation and law enforcement foresaw grave difficulties in maintaining even minimum standards of cleanliness and order.

---

[19] Chicago Park District Code, Chapter 17-27. This ordinance was challenged in Federal Court. The plaintiffs themselves dismissed the suit.

What Limitations to Place on Assemblies and Marches

As has been previously detailed, the City of Chicago was disposed to grant all reasonable requests for permits to assemble and march to demonstrate opposition to the conduct of the war. The petitioning groups did not want to assemble or march anywhere except to and around the Amphitheatre, which request was unreasonable because of the size and duration of the marches proposed and the security measures necessary on the Convention premises. Alternatives were offered. The only specific request for an assembly area which was accepted was for the Grant Park Band Shell on Wednesday, August 28. It was after this assembly, as a matter of fact, that the protesters massed at the Hilton directly across the street from Grant Park and the major disorder occurred.

Whether to Call the Illinois National Guard

The Mayor and other city officals were constantly aware of the great responsibility which they had to protect the safety of the candidates, the delegates and the millions of citizens and visitors who would be present in Chicago during the week of the Convention. Large demonstrations were expected. Wednesday, August 28th had even been pin pointed by Police Intelligence. Since the authorities were fully aware of the past performance of many of the leaders of the dissident groups planning to come to Chicago in turning demonstrations into riots, it was clearly necessary to be prepared for this eventuality. According to the report of the National Advisory Commission on Civil Disorders (Kerner Report):

> "Outside forces will need a relatively long lead time before response. A survey of National Guard capabilities, for example, shows that an average of four to six hours is required from time of notification to the time of arrival of an effective complement of men . . . local authorities must not wait until the critical moment to alert the National Guard."[20]

The recently released Report of the Chicago Riot Study Committee (Austin Report) also stated:

> "In emergency situations in the future the National Guard should be called at the earliest practicable time and the police should not hesitate to recommend such calls. . . ."[21]

---

[20] Kerner Report, Bantam Book Edition, page 488.
[21] Austin Report, page 115.

and from the same report:

> "Police department civil disorder procedures and poli-
> cies, including those related to the use of the Illinois Army
> National Guard and federal troops should be reviewed to
> be certain that they satisfy the fundamental proposition
> that *responses to civil disorders must be met with over-
> whelming manpower and not with firepower....*"[22]

These guidelines are reiterated in a survey of law enforcement officials conducted by *U.S. News and World Report:*

> Raymond Momboisse, deputy attorney general of
> California and author of police manuals and training
> texts for handling riots ... "Police must learn to
> move very rapidly into a riot area. It takes tremen-
> dous manpower." Col. Jacob W. Schott, the chief of
> police of Cincinnati, Ohio: "No police department in
> the country has enough policemen when a riot really
> gets started ... many departments are afraid to
> move in and use necessary force until things are out
> of hand." ... Professor Philip B. Kurland, University
> of Chicago Law School asks "How do you arrest a
> mob? There is a problem of taking away those ar-
> rested and still maintaining police lines. Part of the
> problem is logistics—having enough men to confront
> large numbers of rioters in unexpected situations. I
> know of no way of meeting anarchy other than by
> force. This requires substantial numbers of troops in-
> stantly available. No city can afford the number of po-
> lice needed to handle massive outbreaks such as in De-
> troit and Newark. There's the problem of economics,
> and of our unwillingness to live in a police state with
> troops on every corner 24 hours a day. But we may
> be forced to. Quick, aggressive action by the police
> will lessen blood shed." Philip M. Hauser, professor of
> sociology at the University of Chicago: "There is no al-
> ternative to using whatever superior force is necessary to
> restore order. Either that, or we have anarchy—not a
> society. From Julian Levi, professor of urban affairs at
> the University of Chicago: "It has been repeatedly dem-
> onstrated that the only way you can control an escalat-
> ing riot is to provide the most visible public power you
> can. And you must be willing to use force if it is
> required—though it should be made very clear that it
> will be used impartially. More mistakes are made by

---

[22] *Ibid.* page 45.

delaying the calling up of the Guard than in calling it too soon."[23]

The Chicago Police Department numbers 12,000 men. Even with leaves cancelled and working 12 hour shifts, only part of this complement of men can be available at any given period and this number must continue all the normal law enforcement activities necessary in the City in addition to the special assignment. For this reason the decision was made to call the Guard. It must be recalled that at the time these arrangements had to be made, the authorities could have no way of knowing the actual number of persons who would participate in the various demonstrations nor how many of these latter would occur or in which widely scattered areas.

Public Reactions

Unfortunately it appears that the news media generally attributed malice to the authorities while presuming good will and sincerity on the part of the protesters. This is all the more inexplicable when it is recalled that it has largely been through the news media that the intentions and exploits of the dissidents have been documented over the preceding nine months. The local news media are beginning to show some aspects of what has come to be called "The Other Side" but ugly and distasteful scenes have been reported all over the nation and the world without sufficient explanation to allow the reports to be placed in perspective.

Citizens of the city have manifested overwhelming support of the civil authorities in letters and calls to City Hall. As of September 4, the letters and wires opened and read indicate that 41,185 persons support the Mayor and the Chicago Police Department while 4,290 did not approve their action. The mail is arriving at the rate of approximately 6,000 to 8,000 letters per day.

CONCLUSION

This report is offered not as a defense of the City of Chicago but primarily in an effort to point out the nature and strategy of confrontation as it was employed in Chicago.

We have examined what actually transpired in the city as well as what had been forecast and threatened for the week.

---

[23] United States News and World Report, August 7, 1968, "Anarchy growing threat to big cities", page 30.

The leaders of the dissident movement are nationally known agitators who had arrived fresh from triumphs at Berkeley and Columbia. Their publicly stated purpose in coming to Chicago was twofold. The immediate object was to disrupt the Convention and the City. Their ultimate goal, also publicly proclaimed, was to topple what they consider to be the corrupt institutions of our society, educational, governmental, etc., by impeding and if possible halting their normal functions while exposing the authorities to ridicule and embarrassment. They are anxious to destroy these institutions, but it is unclear as to what replacements they envision, as Senator Daniel Inouye of Hawaii observed in the Convention's Keynote address when he asked "what trees do they plant?"

The dual goals of immediate disruption and ultimate destruction were pursued in Chicago against the government under the guise of a protest against the war in Vietnam. This promised to be a very successful ploy since, as debates at the Convention demonstrated, everyone wants peace and disagreement occurs only over methods.

In spite of such attractive bait, the guerrilla or pyschological warfare tactics which were employed by these revolutionaries erupted in few serious incidents, the main one being an eighteen minute encounter in front of the Hilton Hotel. As is so often the case, the trusting, the innocent, and the idealist were taken in and taken over. The news media too responded with surprising naivete and were incredibly misused. Indeed, any success the revolutionaries achieved in their ultimate objective of fomenting hatred and ridicule among the citizenry against the authorities was in large part attributable to the almost totally sympathetic coverage extended by reporters to the revolutionary leaders and more understandably, to the attractive idealistic but unwary young people who unwittingly lent them assistance and camouflage.

For us in Chicago, the aftermath will involve investigations and assessment of the performance of governmental officials, police and military units, radio, television and newspapers. We are concerned about injured newsmen, injured policemen, injured civilians, injured protesters, injured reputations, but most of all we are concerned about the lack of public awareness of the significance of the departing words of the Yippie and "Mob" leaders, "We won" and "The revolution has begun."

It seems clear that a nucleus of adult trouble makers

avowedly seeking a hostile confrontation with the police will be engaging in the same activities detailed in this report in other cities and towns across the nation. They have announced their intention "to create 200 to 300 Chicagos." All who believe in the essential desirability of our present form of government are challenged to find the best response to what is frequently a violent and revolutionary attack upon our institutions—a response at once effective yet consistent with the dignity and freedom of each and all our citizens.

APPENDIX II

The following Foreward and Summary are excerpted from Rights in Conflict, *The Walker Report to The National Commission on the Causes and Prevention of Violence. The Report was published in December 1968.*

FOREWORD

The right to dissent is fundamental to democracy. But the expression of that right has become one of the most serious problems in contemporary democratic government. That dilemma was dramatized in Chicago during the Democratic National Convention in 1968—the dilemma of a city coping with the expression of dissent.

Unlike other recent big city riots, including those in Chicago itself, the events of convention week did not consist of looting and burning, followed by mass arrests. To a shocking extent they consisted of crowd-police battles in the parks as well as the streets. And the shock was intensified by the presence in the crowds (which included some anarchists and revolutionaries) of large numbers of innocent dissenting citizens.

The initial response, precipitated by dramatic television coverage, was a horrified condemnation of city and police. When demonstrators compared the Chicago police to the Soviet troops then occupying Prague, news commentators sympathetically relayed that comparison to the world. Not since Birmingham and Selma had there been so heated a mood of public outrage.

An immediate counterresponse, however, expressed the feeling that the demonstrators got what they deserved, and the thinking that the city had no alternative. Many observers thought that, in view of the provocation and the circumstances, police had performed admirably and with restraint.

The commentary far outlasted the convention. Major writers in some of the world's most respected periodicals denounced the city, the police, and the Democratic leaders. For its part, the City of Chicago issued "The Strategy of Confrontation," a paper detailing the threat to the city, itemizing provocations, describing a battery of bizarre weapons allegedly intended for use against law enforcement officers, and charging the American news media with biased coverage. The city also prepared a one-hour film shown nationally on television.

These conflicting responses, and the nature of the dilemma imposed upon Chicago, make this study necessary. Our purpose is to present the facts so that thoughtful readers can decide what lessons come out of them; for it is urgent that any such lessons be speedily incorporated into American public life. The *Chicago Tribune* began its special report on convention week with the line, "Not everyone wins." They might have added that there are circumstances in which *no one* wins, in which everyone loses. Such circumstances make up this report.

We have addressed ourselves to questions like the following. What were the objectives of the planned demonstrations, and who planned them? How did the city prepare itself? What types of people made up the crowds in the parks? Were physical and verbal attacks typical of demonstrator behavior? And did they precipitate police violence or follow it? Was the clubbing done by a few tired policemen goaded into "overreacting," or was there large-scale police brutality? Is there evidence that newsmen were singled out for assault? Was Chicago itself conducive to violence, or was it merely where the convention, and the cameras, happened to be?

We believe we have laid a factual foundation for meaningful answers to those questions.

Our charge was not to decide what ought to have been done, or to balance the rights and wrongs, or to recommend a course of action for the future. Having sought out the facts, we intend to let them speak for themselves. But we urge the reader, in assessing these facts, to bear in mind that the physical confrontations in Chicago will be repeated elsewhere until we learn to deal with the dilemma they represent.

In principle at least, most Americans acknowledge the right to dissent. And, in principle at least, most dissenters acknowledge the right of a city to protect its citizens and its property. But what happens when these undeniable rights are brought—deliberately by some—into conflict?

Convention week in Chicago is what happens, and the challenge it brings is plain: to keep *peaceful assembly* from becoming contraction in terms.

A SUMMARY

During the week of the Democratic National Convention, the Chicago police were the target of mounting provocation by both word and act. It took the form of obscene epithets, and of rocks, sticks, bathroom tiles and even human feces hurled at police by demonstrators. Some of these acts had been planned; others were spontaneous or were themselves provoked by police action. Furthermore, the police had been put on edge by widely published threats of attempts to disrupt both the city and the Convention.

That was the nature of the provocation. The nature of the response was unrestrained and indiscriminate police violence on many occasions, particularly at night.

That violence was made all the more shocking by the fact that it was often inflicted upon persons who had broken no law, disobeyed no order, made no threat. These included peaceful demonstrators, onlookers, and large numbers of residents who were simply passing through, or happened to live in, the areas where confrontations were occurring.

Newsmen and photographers were singled out for assault, and their equipment deliberately damaged. Fundamental police training was ignored; and officers, when on the scene, were often unable to control their men. As one police officer put it: "What happened didn't have anything to do with police work."

The violence reached its culmination on Wednesday night.

A report prepared by an inspector from the Los Angeles Police Department, present as an official observer, while generally praising the police restraint he had observed in the parks during the week, said this about the events that night:

> "There is no question but that many officers acted without restraint and exerted force beyond that necessary under the circumstances. The leadership at the point of conflict did little to prevent such conduct and the direct control of officers by first line supervisors was virtually non-existent."

He is referring to the police-crowd confrontation in front of the Conrad Hilton Hotel. Most Americans know about it, having seen the 17-minute sequence played and replayed on their television screens.

But most Americans do not know that the confrontation was followed by even more brutal incidents in the Loop side streets. Or that it had been preceded by comparable instances of indiscriminate police attacks on the North Side a few nights earlier when demonstrators were cleared from Lincoln Park and pushed into the streets and alleys of Old Town.

How did it start? With the emergence long before convention week of three factors which figured significantly in the outbreak of violence. These were: threats to the city; the city's response; and the conditioning of Chicago police to expect that violence against demonstrators, as against rioters, would be condoned by city officials.

The threats to the City were varied. Provocative and inflammatory statements, made in connection with activities planned for convention week, were published and widely disseminated. There were also intelligence reports from informants.

Some of this information was absurd, like the reported plan to contaminate the city's water supply with LSD. But some were serious; and both were strengthened by the authorities' lack of any mechanism for distinguishing one from the other.

The second factor—the city's response—matched, in numbers and logistics at least, the demonstrators' threats.

The city, fearful that the "leaders" would not be able to control their followers, attempted to discourage an inundation of demonstrators by not granting permits for marches and rallies and by making it quite clear that the "law" would be enforced.

Government—federal, state and local—moved to defend itself from the threats, both imaginary and real. The preparations were detailed and far ranging: from stationing firemen at each alarm box within a six block radius of the Amphitheatre to staging U.S. Army armored personnel carriers in Soldier Field under Secret Service control. Six thousand Regular Army troops in full field gear, equipped with rifles, flame throwers, and bazookas were airlifted to Chicago on Monday, August 26. About 6,000 Illinois National Guard troops had already been activated to assist the 12,000 member Chicago Police Force.

Of course, the Secret Service could never afford to ignore threats of assassination of Presidential candidates. Neither could the city, against the background of riots in 1967 and 1968, ignore the ever-present threat of ghetto riots, possibly sparked by large numbers of demonstrators, during convention week.

The third factor emerged in the city's position regarding

the riots following the death of Dr. Martin Luther King and the April 27th peace march to the Civic Center in Chicago.

The police were generally credited with restraint in handling the first riots—but Mayor Daley rebuked the Superintendent of Police. While it was later modified, his widely disseminated "shoot to kill arsonists and shoot to maim looters" order undoubtedly had an effect.

The effect on police became apparent several weeks later, when they attacked demonstrators, bystanders and media representatives at a Civic Center peace march. There were published criticisms—but the city's response was to ignore the police violence.

That was the background. On August 18, 1968, the advance contingent of demonstrators arrived in Chicago and established their base, as planned, in Lincoln Park on the city's Near North Side. Throughout the week, they were joined by others—some from the Chicago area, some from states as far away as New York and California. On the weekend before the convention began, there were about 2,000 demonstrators in Lincoln Park; the crowd grew to about 10,000 by Wednesday.

There were, of course, the hippies—the long hair and love beads, the calculated unwashedness, the flagrant banners, the open lovemaking and disdain for the constraints of conventional society. In dramatic effect, both visual and vocal, these dominated a crowd whose members actually differed widely in physical appearance, in motivation, in political affiliation, in philosophy. The crowd included Yippies come to "do their thing," youngsters working for a political candidate, professional people with dissenting political views, anarchists and determined revolutionaries, motorcycle gangs, black activists, young thugs, police and secret service undercover agents. There were demonstrators waving the Viet Cong flag and the red flag of revolution and there were the simply curious who came to watch and, in many cases, became willing or unwilling participants.

To characterize the crowd, then, as entirely hippy-Yippie, entirely "New Left," entirely anarchist, or entirely youthful political dissenters is both wrong and dangerous. The stereotyping that did occur helps to explain the emotional reaction of both police and public during and after the violence that occurred.

Despite the presence of some revolutionaries, the vast majority of the demonstrators were intent on expressing by peaceful means their dissent either from society generally or from the administration's policies in Vietnam.

Most of those intending to join the major protest demonstrations scheduled during convention week did not plan to enter the Amphitheatre and disrupt the proceedings of the Democratic convention, did not plan aggressive acts of physical provocation against the authorities, and did not plan to use rallies of demonstrators to stage an assault against any person, institution, or place of business. But while it is clear that most of the protesters in Chicago had no intention of initiating violence, this is not to say that they did not expect it to develop.

It was the clearing of the demonstrators from Lincoln Park that led directly to the violence: symbolically, it expressed the city's opposition to the protesters; literally, it forced the protesters into confrontation with police in Old Town and the adjacent residential neighborhoods.

The Old Town area near Lincoln Park was a scene of police ferocity exceeding that shown on television on Wednesday night. From Sunday night through Tuesday night, incidents of intense and indiscriminate violence occurred in the streets after police had swept the park clear of demonstrators.

Demonstrators attacked too. And they posed difficult problems for police as they persisted in marching through the streets, blocking traffic and intersections. But it was the police who forced them out of the park and into the neighborhood. And on the part of the police there was enough wild club swinging, enough cries of hatred, enough gratuitous beating to make the conclusion inescapable that individual policemen, and lots of them, committed violent acts far in excess of the requisite force for crowd dispersal or arrest. To read dispassionately the hundreds of statements describing at firsthand the events of Sunday and Monday nights is to become convinced of the presence of what can only be called a police riot.

Here is an eyewitness talking about Monday night:

"The demonstrators were forced out onto Clark Street and once again a traffic jam developed. Cars were stopped, the horns began to honk, people couldn't move, people got gassed inside their cars, people got stoned inside their cars, police were the objects of stones, and taunts, mostly taunts. As you must understand, most of the taunting of the police was verbal.

There were stones thrown of course, but for the most part it was verbal. But there were stones being thrown and of course the police were responding with tear gas and clubs and everytime they could get near enough to a demonstrator they hit him.

"But again you had this police problem within—this really turned into a police problem. They pushed everybody out of the park, but this night there were a lot more people in the park than there had been during the previous night and Clark Street was just full of people and in addition now was full of gas because the police were using gas on a much larger scale this night. so the police were faced with the task, which took them about an hour or so, of hitting people over the head and gassing them enough to get them out of Clark Street, which they did."

But police action was not confined to the necessary force, even in clearing the park:

A young man and his girl friend were both grabbed by officers. He screamed, "We're going, we're going," but they threw him into the pond. The officers grabbed the girl, knocked her to the ground, dragged her along the embankment and hit her with their batons on her head, arms, back and legs. The boy tried to scramble up the embankment to her, but police shoved him back in the water at least twice. He finally got to her and tried to pull her in the water, away from the police. He was clubbed on the head five or six times. An officer shouted, "Let's get the fucking bastard!" but the boy pulled her into the water and the police left.

Like the incident described above, much of the violence witnessed in Old Town that night seems malicious or mindless:

There were pedestrians. People who were not part of the demonstration were coming out of a tavern to see what the demonstration was . . . and the officers indiscriminately started beating everybody on the street who was not a policeman.

Another scene:

There was a group of about six police officers that moved in and started beating two youths. When one of the officers pulled back his nightstick to swing, one of the youths grabbed it from behind and started beating on the officer. At this point about ten officers left everybody else and ran after this youth, who turned down Wells and ran to the left.

But the officers went to the right, picked up another youth, assuming he was the one they were chasing, and took him into an empty lot and beat him. And when they got him to the ground, they just kicked him ten times—the wrong youth, the innocent youth who had been standing there.

A federal legal official relates an experience of Tuesday evening.

I then walked one block north where I met a group of 12-15 policemen. I showed them my identification and they permitted me to walk with them. The police walked one block west. Numerous people were watching us from their windows and balconies. The police yelled profanities at them, taunting them to come down where the police would beat them up. The police stopped a number of people on the street demanding identification. They verbally abused each pedestrian and pushed one or two without hurting them. We walked back to Clark Street and began to walk north where the police stopped a number of people who appeared to be protesters, and ordered them out of the area in a very abusive way. One protester who was walking in the opposite direction was kneed in the groin by a policeman who was walking towards him. The boy fell to the ground and swore at the policeman who picked him up and threw him to the ground. We continued to walk toward the command post. A derelict who appeared to be very intoxicated, walked up to the policeman and mumbled something that was incoherent. The policeman pulled from his belt a tin container and sprayed its contents into the eyes of the derelict, who stumbled around and fell on his face.

It was on these nights that the police violence against media representatives reached its peak. Much of it was plainly deliberate. A newsman was pulled aside on Monday by a detective acquaintance of his who said: "The word is being passed to get newsmen." Individual newsmen were warned, "You take my picture tonight and I'm going to get you." Cries of "get the camera" preceded individual attacks on photographers.

A newspaper photographer describes Old Town on Monday at about 9:00 p.m.:

When the people arrived at the intersection of Wells and Division, they were not standing in the streets. Suddenly a column of policemen ran out from the alley. They were reinforcements. They were under control but there seemed to be no direction. One man was yelling, 'Get them up on the sidewalks, turn them around.' Very suddenly the police charged the people on the sidewalks and began beating their heads. A line of cameramen was 'trapped' along with the crowd along the sidewalks, and the police went down the line chopping away at the cameras.

A network cameraman reports that on the same night:

I just saw this guy coming at me with his nightstick and I had the camera up. The tip of his stick hit me right in the mouth, then I put my tongue up there and I noticed that my tooth was gone. I turned around then to try to leave and then this cop came up behind me with his stick and he jabbed me in the back.

All of a sudden these cops jumped out of the police cars and started just beating the hell out of people. And before anything else happened to me, I saw a man holding a Bell & Howell camera with big wide letters on it, saying 'CBS.' He apparently had been hit by a cop. And cops were standing around and there was blood streaming down his face. Another policeman was running after me and saying, 'Get the fuck out of here.' And I heard another guy scream, 'Get their fucking cameras.' And the next thing I know I was being hit on the head, and I think on the back, and I was just forced down on the ground at the corner of Division and Wells.

If the intent was to discourage coverage, it was successful in at least one case. A photographer from a news magazine says that finally, "I just stopped shooting, because every time you push the flash, they look at you and they are screaming about, 'Get the fucking photographers and get the film.' "

There is some explanation for the media-directed violence. Camera crews on at least two occasions did stage violence and fake injuries. Demonstrators did sometimes step up their activities for the benefit of TV cameras. Newsmen and photographers' blinding lights did get in the way of police clearing streets, sweeping the park and dispersing demonstrators. Newsmen did, on occasion, disobey legitimate police orders to "move" or "clear the streets." News reporting of events did seem to the police to be anti-Chicago and anti-police.

But was the response appropriate to the provocation?

Out of 300 newsmen assigned to cover the parks and streets of Chicago during convention week, more than 60 (about 20%) were involved in incidents resulting in injury to themselves, damage to their equipment, or their arrest. Sixty-three newsmen were physically attacked by police; in 13 of these instances, photographic or recording equipment was intentionally damaged.

The violence did not end with either demonstrators or newsmen on the North Side on Sunday, Monday and Tuesday. It continued in Grant Park on Wednesday. It occurred on Michigan Avenue in front of the Conrad Hilton Hotel, as already described. A high-ranking Chicago police commander admits that on that occasion the police "got out of control." This same commander appears in one of the most vivid scenes of the entire week, trying desperately to keep individual policemen from beating demonstrators as he screams, "For Christ's sake, stop it!"

Thereafter, the violence continued on Michigan Avenue and on the side streets running into Chicago's Loop. A federal official describes how it began:

"I heard a 10-1 call [policeman in trouble] on either my radio or one of the other hand sets carried by men with me and then heard 'Car 100—sweep.' With roar of motors, squads, vans and three-wheelers came from east, west and north into the block north of Jackson. The crowd scattered. A big group ran west on Jackson, with a group of blue shirted policeman in pursuit, beating at them with clubs. Some of the crowd would jump into doorways and the police would rout them out. The action was very tough. In my judgment, unnecessarily so. The police were hitting with a vengeance and quite obviously with relish. . . ."

What followed was a club-swinging melee. Police ranged the streets striking anyone they could catch. To be sure, demonstrators threw things at policemen and at police cars; but the weight of violence was overwhelmingly on the side of the police. A few examples will give the flavor of that night in Chicago:

"At the corner of Congress Plaza and Michigan," states a doctor, "was gathered a group of people, numbering between thirty and forty. They were trapped against a railing [along a ramp leading down from Michigan Avenue to an underground parking garage] by several policemen on motorcycles. The police charged the people on motorcycles and struck about a dozen of them, knocking several of them down. About twenty standing there jumped over the railing. On the other side of the railing was a three-to-four-foot drop. None of the people who were struck by the motorcycles appeared to be seriously injured. However, several of them were limping as if they had been run over on their feet."

A UPI reporter witnessed these attacks, too. He relates in his statement that one officer, "with a smile on his face and a fanatical look in his eyes, was standing on a three-wheel cycle, shouting, 'Wahoo, wahoo,' and trying to run down people on the sidewalk." The reporter said he was chased thirty feet by the cycle.

A priest who was in the crowd says he saw a "boy, about fourteen or fifteen, white, standing on top of an automobile yelling something which was unidentifiable. Suddenly a policeman pulled him down from the car and beat him to the ground by striking him three or four times with a nightstick. Other police joined in . . . and they eventually shoved him to a police van.

"A well-dressed woman saw this incident and spoke angrily to a nearby police captain. As she spoke, another policeman came up from behind her and sprayed something in her face with an aerosol can. He then clubbed her to the ground. He and two other policemen then dragged her along the ground to the same paddy wagon and threw her in."

"I ran west on Jackson," a witness states. "West of Wabash, a line of police stretching across both sidewalks and the street charged after a small group I was in. Many people were clubbed and maced as they ran. Some weren't demonstrators at all, but were just pedestrians who didn't know how to react to the charging officers yelling 'Police!' "

"A wave of police charged down Jackson," another witness relates. "Fleeing demonstrators were beaten indiscriminately and a temporary, makeshift first aid station was set up on the corner of State and Jackson. Two men lay in pools of blood, their heads severely cut by clubs. A minister moved amongst the crowd, quieting them, brushing aside curious onlookers, and finally asked a policeman to call an ambulance, which he agreed to do. . . ."

An Assistant U.S. Attorney later reported that "the demonstrators were running as fast as they could but were unable to get out of the way because of the crowds in front of them. I observed the police striking numerous individuals, perhaps 20 to 30. I saw three fall down and then overrun by the

police. I observed two demonstrators who had multiple cuts
on their heads. We assisted one who was in shock into a
passerby's car."

Police violence was a fact of convention week. Were the
policemen who committed it a minority? It appears certain
that they were—but one which has imposed some of the consequences of its actions on the majority, and certainly on their
commanders. There has been no public condemnation of these
violators of sound police procedures and common decency by
either their commanding officers or city officials. Nor (at the
time this Report is being completed—almost three months after
the convention) has any disciplinary action been taken against
most of them. That some policemen lost control of themselves
under exceedingly provocative circumstances can perhaps be
understood; but not condoned. If no action is taken against
them, the effect can only be to discourage the majority of
policemen who acted responsibly, and further weaken the
bond between police and community.

Although the crowds were finally dispelled on the nights
of violence in Chicago, the problems they represent have not
been. Surely this is not the last time that a violent dissenting
group will clash head-on with those whose duty it is to
enforce the law. And the next time the whole world will still
be watching.

APPENDIX III

William Good and Jeffrey St. John foresaw the strategy of militant groups and the impending explosion at the Democratic Convention in Chicago. Their article "Ballots or Bullets?" appeared in Barron's National Business & Financial Weekly *on August 19, 1968, one week before the Chicago riots.* *

BALLOTS OR BULLETS?

Radical Leftists May Trigger Violence Next Week in Chicago

By William Good
And Jeffrey St. John

This week, as all the world knows, Democrats and "democrats" of every stripe will begin making their way to Chicago. Residents of the Windy City may be forgiven if they regard the prospect with mixed emotions, for if nothing else things ought to be livelier during the party's National Convention than they were for Republicans at Miami Beach a fortnight ago. To be sure, the name of Spiro Agnew, if "not a household word" (as the G.O.P Vice Presidential candidate was happy to admit), did turn out to be something of a sputtering bombshell when it first was dropped several miles away in a Miami ghetto; meanwhile, blacks and whites were shooting it up over issues none too distinct but, apparently, not related to the presence of Mr. Agnew and his fellow visitors across the bay. In general, calm and sunshine prevailed at Miami Beach. By contrast, Chicago promises to be both windy and hot.

The Yippies Are Coming

Upwards of 100,000 militant radicals, ranging from student groups and so-called Yippies to out-and-out Black Power zealots, are expected to converge on the convention site. Security precautions approaching those of a police state have been implemented by Democratic chiefs at the city, state and

*This article reprinted courtesy of *Barron's National Business & Financial Weekly*.

federal level. Nevertheless, reports persist that a carefully organized civic disturbance of major (perhaps unprecedented) proportions will be touched off by a handful of self-styled American Marxists.

The city that almost burned down once before makes an ominous convention site for the party in power today. Such incendiary plans for revolutionary disruption, after all, are set against a backdrop of racial violence that Mayor Richard Daley's dedicated legions somehow have been unable to control; prominent among the city's trouble-making groups are the so-called Blackstone Rangers, of recent contempt-of-Congress notoriety. Adding fuel to the fire in the next few days is sure to be a delegate-seating challenge from the rump Loyal Democrats of Mississippi, headed by Charles Evers (and backed by Hubert Humphrey). There is every indication, then, that the white radicals now heading for Chicago hope their scheme of disruption will ignite widespread rioting, looting and sniping on a scale dwarfing that of recent incidents in Cleveland or Miami.

If all this comes as a rude shock, it shouldn't. The intentions and goals of domestic Marxist revolutionaries have been well documented (in *Barron's*, for example, by Alice Widener and other writers). The problem is that such warnings largely have been ignored by government and the communications media. The Democrats in convention assembled could find their chickens coming home to roost, since the target will be the very party which has held sway in Washington since U.S. riots began breaking out five years ago. On the unofficial agenda at Chicago, therefore, may be the first brutal attempt by American radicals to force political decisions through mob violence, or the threat of it—the beginning of a new phase in America's revolutionary war of the 'Sixties.

The rough blueprint for disruption at the Democratic Convention was spelled out at a June 29 press conference, in New York City, held by the Fifth Avenue Parade Committee. On hand to launch the Chicago-bound National Mobilization Committee (MOB) was its chairman—and leader of the bloody October 1967 March on the Pentagon—David Dellinger, who likes to call himself "a non-Soviet Communist." Present, too, was Tom Hayden, a founder of Students for a Democratic Society (SDS), who, between and since trips to Hanoi (with fellow traveling Yale Professor Staughton Lynd and U.S. Communist theoretician

Herbert Aptheker), has led a number of the SDS street scenes.

Making MOB's Scene

MOB's battle plan is as simple as it is sinister: the aim is to bring convention machinery to a halt for "failing to serve the human needs of the people." Helping in this endeavor will be the hippie-derivative group called Yippies. Jerry Rubin, the head Yippie, doubles as leader of the Peking-leaning Progressive Labor Party (PLP) and was Dellinger's "co-project director" for last year's Pentagon affair.

PLP boasts a record of achievements and stated goals all its own. First, its vice chairman, William Epton, got himself convicted for inciting the 1964 Harlem riots. Second, PLP appears to be muscling into control of SDS by infiltration, pushing out many of the well-meaning but "misguided" (non-Marxist) members. Third, as its national student organizer, Jeff Gordon, bluntly told the radical newsweekly *Guardian* (July 6, 1968): "We in the PLP are inspired by revolutionaries all over the world who use (Marxism-Leninism) successfully to win Socialism. Yes, in this context we are very proud to be 'Peking-oriented.' Our orientation is for smashing state power of U.S. imperialism and replacing it with the working class."

The Flower Children

But are the Yippies an extension of PLP? Not quite, as New York's underground publication *East Village Other* has reported. They "are the children of the middle class; children who refuse to 'grow up,' refuse to accept the world their parents created. The Yippies have had white-middle-class America, and they didn't like it." To many observers, the hippie sub-culture, popularized as benign by the mass media, sooner or later had to drop in on active radical politics.

Yippies got into the act last March 20, with a "Yip-in" at New York's bustling Grand Central Terminal. Boldly blocking passengers and trains, while battling police, 5,000 Yippies disrupted the station for two and a half hours. Some observers have suggested that the "Yip-in" was a dry run for the Democratic Convention, since Jerry Rubin even then had been writing about his plan to disrupt the Chicago conclave. Recently, the Yippie office confided that it hopes to put 10,000 erstwhile flower children into the Windy City. Rennie Davis, MOB coordinator and a Dellinger associate, said in a telephone interview that Rubin's group is "closely cooperating" with the MOB.

Silly-sounding as all this may seem, a closer look at what
MOB and Yippies plan for the Democrats can dispel any hu-
mor in the situation. Indeed, it must be causing the stoical
Mayor Daley to shudder. Tom Hayden spelled things out in
his June 29 press conference, as quoted by *Guardian*. "We are
planning tactics of prolonged direct action to put heat on the
government and its political party." In New Left rhetoric,
"direct action" can include street barricading, fire bombing,
seizure of buildings and massive confrontations with the
police. Last spring's siege of Columbia University, which
Hayden helped to lead, hinted at what's to come for Chicago.

"We realize that it will be no picnic," Hayden says, "but
responsibility for any violence that develops lies with the authorities, not the demonstrators." Hayden means, of course,
that Chicago police must not stop his shock troops if they
invade the convention hall, block traffic or make exits and
entrances impossible. Such tactics, refined at Columbia, were
tested first at the Pentagon. Here's how a national newsmaga-
zine described the earlier scene: "An assault squad wielding
clubs and ax handles probed the rope barriers in front of the
Pentagon entrances, taunting and testing white-hatted federal
marshals who stood in close line. After 90-odd minutes of
steadily rising invective and rolling around in the north parking
lot of the Pentagon, flying wedges of demonstrators surged
toward the less heavily defended press entrances."

Ten of the "peace protestors" actually managed to penetrate the Pentagon. With their ranks greatly swelled in Chicago, how many more might gain access to the convention
floor, even physically taking it over? More than a hundred
anti-war groups mustered for the march on the Pentagon
produced a mob force estimated at 55,000. For Chicago, that
number easily could double or triple. On June 29, both
Dellinger and Hayden stated that most of the organizations
present at the Pentagon will return for the Convention. The
latter-day Yippies, for their part, marshalled 5,000 at Grand
Central. How many can they dredge up in a nationwide
effort, presumably recruited from New York, San Francisco,
Boston and other hippie haunts? All told, the motley crowd
converging on Chicago could number a quarter-million.

East Village Other has given a glimpse of what the Yippies,
at least, have in mind. As a starter, brothers and sisters
dressed in Viet Cong garb will go "electioneering," shaking
hands in mimicry of bourgeois politicians. Others even will go

to work, if only temporarily. "Yippies plan to paint their cars like taxicabs, pick up delegates and drop them off in Wisconsin," observes the underground publication. "We are infiltrating the hotels with bellboys and cooks. We are also infiltrating the press." Sound like innocent child's play for the flower children? "The Democrats," reports E.V.O., "will probably have to travel from hotel to convention hall by helicopter."

Last November 16, Jerry Rubin summed up the strategy for disruption, in *The Village Voice*, with this clarion call: "See you next August in Chicago at the Democratic National convention. Bring pot, fake delegates' cards, smokebombs, costumes, blood to throw, and all kinds of interesting props. Also football helmets."

No Tea Party?

It's clear that Chicago is in for something more serious than a panty raid. The possibility of arousing ghetto violence, moreover, is quite real. Here's Rubin, in *The Village Voice*: "The goal? A massive white revolutionary youth movement which, working in parallel cooperation with the rebellions in the black communities, could seriously disrupt this country, and thus be an internal catalyst for a breakdown of the American ability and will to fight guerrillas overseas. Thus defeated abroad by peasant revolutionaries, and disrupted from within by blacks and whites, the empire of the United States will find itself faced with rebellions from fifteen different directions."

Further, according to Hayden, "in the future it is conceivable that students will threaten destruction of buildings as the last deterrent to police attacks." It follows that both Rubin and Hayden actually need the police, to oppose the radicals in a forceful confrontation. No longer pretending concern with simple issues (like Columbia's education reform or opposition to the draft), their interest is in the inciting of violence as a political weapon. Such tactics, not incidentally, also tend to gain new recruits to their ranks. After SDS' June convention, FBI Director J. Edgar Hoover observed that a "sabotage-explosive workshop even discussed the finer points of firing Molotov cocktails from shotguns, as well as similar forms of so-called defense measures that could be used in defiance of police action."

The new development within the white radical camp not only points to violence, but also to the "glory of death" in "confrontations" on behalf of the "cause." If this seems a dubious assumption, here's what the New Left publication, *Ramparts,* had to say about the Pentagon riot: "Objectively speaking, perhaps the best thing that could have happened . . . would have been for somebody to have been killed. For American soldiers to have shot unarmed American civilians exercising their right of free speech would have been a blow from which the Administration could never recover."

Children's Crusade

Dragged into this potentially Draconian nightmare may be Senator Eugene McCarthy's youthful horde of idealistic supporters—the celebrated "Children's Crusade." While many adult McCarthy boosters are aware of the MOB and Yippie threat, few of the well-meaning college students seem willing to believe they could become unwitting pawns. (There's evidence that Senator McCarthy does; last week he asked them all to stay home and "demonstrate in your own cities." His self-appointed field leader, Allard Lowenstein, indicated he wouldn't take orders of that sort.)

Great numbers of these young people almost certainly will go to Chicago. Clinton Deveaux, McCarthy's convention coordinator has indicated that a *Life* magazine estimate of one million McCarthyites in Chicago was too low; until recently, he had hopes for 1½ or even two million. "Anybody that wants to go will go," shrugs another staffer. "If they have to beg or borrow their way. There will be more people than that city has ever seen. These are kids who slept on desks and who actually went hungry during the New York primary."

Emotionally, the campaign is do-or-die for many of McCarthy's young people. However misplaced their response, it nonetheless makes for still another potentially explosive threat overhanging the Convention. Although McCarthy's kids may be nonviolent in nature, the followers of Dellinger, Rubin & Co. plan to try enlisting the McCarthy supporters in their disruption, by means of "pre-convention" demonstrations in favor of the Minnesota Senator.

If McCarthy loses his bid for the nomination, what happens? His youthful followers likely would conclude that "the system is corrupt." Those radical pre-convention agitations then could evolve into a "protest march," which in turn could mushroom into a full-blown riot. Some McCarthy activists already have threatened to "disrupt" if Vice President Humphrey is the nominee. Pete Hamill, in *The Village Voice* (June 20) warned: "It is as simple as this: It must be McCarthy, because it can't be Humphrey. If the Central Committee (the Democratic Convention delegates) gives us Humphrey anyway, we can drift into quietism, and tend our private garden, or we can disrupt, disrupt, disrupt."

Ironically, then, the radical revolutionaries win if Humphrey does. He is heir apparent to the Johnson Administration policies. No matter how much he has tried to pull away in recent months, Mr. Humphrey is the "evil symbol of the establishment" the radicals need to keep them in business.

On the other hand, if McCarthy somehow were to win, the radicals would be in real trouble. First, as the May 20 issue of the SDS publication *New Left Notes* lamented, student support for the radicals was drained away by the active campaigns of both Senator McCarthy and the late Senator Robert Kennedy. This drain could be permanent, eliminating an important segment of radical support, if the "system" actually works to produce a McCarthy nomination. That would prove the radicals wrong and the liberals right—precipitating a grave crisis in radical ranks.

Precedent de Gaulle

Proof of the validity of such a contention has been supplied by New Left Professor Staughton Lynd. Using as a point of reference de Gaulle's use of the political process to defuse what French radicals started last May, Lynd wrote in the July 13 *Guardian*: "American radicals will be pondering the lessons of the French experience for a long time to come. One thing seems clear: the use of the electoral process to defuse, co-opt, and emasculate confrontation politics has been classically demonstrated."

In reality, the radicals, hoping for violent confrontation at Chicago, desperately want a Humphrey victory—to block McCarthy, who seems to represent a more dangerous threat to their future than anyone else on the American political scene today. They need anger, frustration and hostility from McCarthy's supporters. Thus, an imperative for MOB and Yippie leaders is to precipitate disruptive "Demonstrations for McCarthy," hoping any accompanying violence will frighten the delegates at Chicago's stockyards into a stampede to Humphrey.

How Mayor Daley, his Chicago police, the Illinois troopers

and the national Democratic Party officials will react to such a series of events remains to be seen. McCarthy's willingness to take second place on the ticket with Humphrey might offer a way around the worst of the impending trouble. But there's no question that Chicago provides an ideal combination of incendiary factors, and the Democratic Convention offers the spark to touch it off.